AF248624

The Answer

A. Lou Alphin

VIRGINIA BEACH
CAPE CHARLES

Dedication

To my Christian parents and grandparents, for the example of God's love they modeled for me growing up as a child.

To my late husband, whom I will always love, he was a gift and a blessing from God for nearly thirty-nine years of marriage.

To my family and friends, you have enriched my life with your love.

And most of all to Jesus Christ, what an unselfish sacrifice made on the cross over 2,000 years ago! It is to your *name* and you as the *Son of God*, our *Savior*, that I share this personal invitation to the world to believe and trust that you are the answer.

Introduction

I AM A sixty-three-year-old widow of five years. The loves of my life are my two grown sons, my daughter-in-law, and my three grandsons. All other family members are gifts from God as well. I love each one of them. I have cherished friends from my days in kindergarten, from my hometown in North Carolina, and from my life in Virginia Beach. I am grateful to have lived a full and blessed life. One of the wishes on my bucket list was to write this book to tell of my personal words of knowledge that I have received and experienced over the last forty-plus years and to give insight by sharing my gift received through God.

My life is most likely not much different than yours, and I am not a perfect human. I do not claim to be perfect. I am a work in progress daily. I will use the words "I" or "me" to let you know what I have learned. I will use the words "you," "our," or "us" because I want to include *everyone,* as readers, with this invitation to experience and be part of this journey. I will use "you" at the beginning of some invitational and requests sentences, which is not meant to be a command or demand at all. "You" will be used only for you to know that "you" is understood. I write in this manner to speak to each individual, as well as to speak to all of you, as if we are sitting around talking comfortably as a group of believers and nonbelievers about this book called *The Answer.* I will begin by saying that I am a Christian, and

Jesus is my answer to any question or problem. To me, Jesus is my everything because I desire to have a personal partnership with *him*. I know that as long as I believe and am in relationship with Jesus and speaking his name, I am evolving to know our very creator. As a Christian, I want fellowship with Jesus. It is not religion but the desire for spiritual intimacy with Jesus. Is Jesus everything to you? Do you know Jesus personally and as your partner through life? Are you in daily fellowship with Jesus? Jesus wants to hear from you and me daily. We, as Christians, are to *glorify* his name. We are his daily witnesses for our beloved Savior, Jesus. He is each breath we will ever breathe; he is our giver of life.

Although I have no formal religious education, while growing up I listened to Bible stories in Sunday school and during Sunday morning sermons. I am thankful to have heard the word of God at an early age. My greatest love is the gift of knowing and believing in Jesus Christ: the Father, the Son, and the Holy Spirit. This is the Trinity. The Trinity is believed to be the three in *one*. The three are united and holy as *One*.

God has been prompting me to write this book for a long time, and it is of the utmost importance in my life that I obey that calling. The purpose of writing this book is to share my journey with Jesus and the personal words of knowledge God has gifted me with over the last forty-plus years. My prayer is that through this book you will gain insight, be inspired, and be encouraged in your walk with the Lord. The message is simple: Jesus is our answer. There is no other answer ever for mankind.

I believe religion is comprised of rituals, routines, and believing that our good works, our human acts, and our performances by our self-effort are the pathway to knowing God. That is not what this book is endorsing. This book is about Christianity, not religion. Christianity is a daily process of evolving to be Christlike in our thoughts, choices, and actions every moment of every day. As we learn to submit ourselves to Jesus, we evolve to become more like Jesus. We are a work in progress throughout each moment we live. It is we, as humans, submitting our will to the will of God, to Jesus through to our Father. God is our Father, Jesus is the Son, and the Holy Spirit is the three in *one* that lives within each of us. When I write about

Jesus, I am not forgetting our Father or the Holy Spirit. To me, when I think or speak of Jesus, I hold our Father and the Holy Spirit within my heart. I could not think or speak about Jesus without our Father and the Holy Spirit being acknowledged as well. Through Jesus, we do have access to our Father who teaches us through his Holy Spirit. You can see why Jesus is always our answer.

Jesus wants all of his people to know him, his truth, and his love. The answer and truth is that, as Christians, we need to renew our minds daily to who Jesus is to us in the world God created. God will renew our minds, our hearts, our spirits, our souls, and our physical bodies daily as we yearn for and evolve toward our own personal relationship with God through Jesus. This personal relationship enlightens us to our self-worth and to the empowerment of who we are in the knowledge that God lives within us.

Our conscious mind exists within our every inner thought that is deep within our brains. However, I am using the word *conscience* in this writing to go to a deeper or higher level as believers, to hold your and my thoughts to his Christlike standard. God's biblical principles are proof of his morals and ethics for Christians through all generations and today. That is the difference I want to establish between these two words. Wouldn't it be nice for all of us to join in the global *collective conscience and love* for the betterment of mankind? As the author of this book, I am asking all people in God's universe to consider Jesus in the year 2015 and the years to come, please; Why? This is not a Pollyanna request. We have the answer right before our eyes: Jesus. Why do we ignore the fact Jesus is always our answer?

An important element in the process of becoming Christlike is to *consciously* and regularly remember and speak the name of Jesus out loud. The name Jesus is truth, light, and love, which is the answer needed desperately by all today. You read the Bible, and you learn of his holy promises. You acknowledge his presence when you witness his words and promises fulfilled during each day of your life. You fall in love with Jesus, and you pray to him, our *Heavenly* Father. He loves us and desires the bond of our peace and the unity of our love together. Jesus is waiting. Think of the name Jesus and who Jesus is to you as well. Jesus's invitation is offered through Jesus who is the Son of God. There is no one ever too far from God.

My prayer is that this book will provide insight and wisdom to help you as you journey toward a personal relationship with God. You will read about my personal relationship with God and my journey from a child and teenager through the last forty-plus years. You will hear about the gift of words of knowledge or what some might call premonitions or revelations that God has given me. I am only sharing what I have been inspired to write with a heartfelt desire for you to discover what I have learned and experienced. You'll notice that I repeat certain words and phrases. I do this deliberately, as I believe, they need to be heard over and over in order to convey the message that God loves you, and you have God's love, power, and authority within you.

From a young child to the present day, the *Spirit of God* taught me that *hope* is part of me. With that *hope* inside me, I discovered more and more about Jesus. On one Sunday morning, I accepted Jesus within my heart. From that moment on, there was no doubt that I knew God's love lived within me. That is a moment I have never forgotten. I repeat *that hope* is within you and me. I pray that during this reading *hope* becomes a part of your thinking, desire, and belief as you search for your own faith through Jesus. The desire needs to be strong and not lukewarm; it is required daily. Constant and consistent *hope* that never falters endures only through the love of Jesus's love, his power, and his authority through God.

You do not let another negative thought of doubt cross your mind to guilt you or condemn you into not believing in God's love for you. With Jesus within your heart and guiding your steps, you will learn to unburden yourself through a renewed mind daily and *consciously*. God wants our daily walk with him to be a joyful journey every moment of every day no matter what the circumstances or situations, which is the ultimate gift of love through God to you and me. The Holy Spirit will be your source of comfort and contentment during your sunny days and your cloudy days. I am not talking about the weather. I am talking about God watching over us to lift us up with his strength that we need to live in this world second by second as humans. You read the Bible, and you meditate on the name Jesus, our *Master Teacher*. He is our answer.

Many people look up to *heaven*, the invisible realm, towards God's kingdom. The same kingdom of the *Spirit of God* is within you, so look inside yourself too. God's *heaven* will be revealed to all of us one day. As believers, Jesus's power and authority is born within each of us. Knowing and wholeheartedly believing in and having a personal relationship with Jesus is the answer to any and all problems we may encounter in this world. Belief is not just on Sundays; belief is every day. The Bible's promises need to be read and brought to mind daily. Because you love Jesus, you will want to read his holy words and promises.

The New Testament teaches about the Son of God, Jesus, and his life on earth with mankind. The New Testament is of Jesus. Jesus is *grace*. Jesus of Nazareth is the gospel of *grace*; this is his life, his death, and his resurrection. God's words and God's promises minister to and instruct believers by providing insight into every aspect of life we may face. You keep your eyes upon him and rest in his peace and safety. He does remain within you forever. Jesus is your answer.

Throughout your journey, you will want to know more about Jesus. Do not suppress this desire; it is an innate longing within us upon birth. With each day, we evolve as believers. It is a process. It is not a one day or forgotten done deal arrangement. The walk with Jesus is a daily and moment-by-moment commitment. Many people give up so quickly on their walk with Jesus. With one discouraging stumbling block or bump in the road, they're done. Why? Because it takes work. It takes desire and intentional devotion to stand steadfast in one's belief. It takes faith, trust, and belief in our *Heavenly* Father to receive the daily and needed answers through the Holy Spirit. I ask Jesus in prayer to teach me about my unbelief and to supply all my needs. The strength Jesus gives me provides such sweet love and joy.

You prayerfully meditate on his words and the name of Jesus, his life, and the sacrifice he made for all mankind. You study his promises in the Bible, and you talk to Jesus in prayer. These daily practices lead to spiritual growth and open the door for his *heavenly* gifts to be manifested. These free gifts from Jesus begin to show up as what we believe to be miracles and answers to prayer. They are not random coincidences. Believe before you actually physically see the manifestations by saying, "I believe to see ________________ coming my way. Thank you, God."

God sees and knows all concerning his children. He knows our hearts and sees our unbelief. Our minds and hearts must not be divided in our belief in Jesus. Doubt and disbelief will be our daily challenge to face as believers. Jesus must be your rock of foundation. We trust Jesus and accept his words and promises, or we do not. It's our choice. God will grow the smallest mustard seed of faith when we trust him, believe in him, and rely on his promises as we continue to develop and desire a personal relationship with him. Believers are raised to reach higher levels that evolve daily and manifest access to Jesus. Each day, Jesus does desire for us to grow in a deeper, more intimate fellowship with him. This is a sealed deal, a one hundred percent committed partnership with him in a Father-child relationship. Receive Jesus as your true Father. He is our only answer!

God wants us to make an honest effort and take responsibility concerning our personal relationship with him. You read your Bible; it's your pathway toward the free access of the gift of the Holy Spirit who is our *heavenly* and individual teacher, our *Master Teacher.* God does not want you to claim ignorance by not knowing his words and his promises through the Bible. Your humble desire to get to know him pleases God. All of us are able to do that for God, aren't we?

Today, the church turns off the majority of people. You ask him to help you find a church and preacher you feel comfortable listening to regularly. It is important to have a church community to fellowship with and grow in your faith. You find a church where you share your faith and connect with other believers. You be patient and ask God for wisdom in finding a church home. I am waiting for revivals to ignite the churches soon. How about you? I believe today we are on the verge of a much-needed *spiritual awakening* to come soon. You consider Jesus, and you accept his love now. These are invitations, not commands or demands.

In my experience, I found people do not consider or believe it's possible for humans to obtain righteousness through Jesus. We are able, and we do. I wanted to know I was righteous and becoming more righteous. I knew God was righteous, however, I was not taught that. As a believer, I evolved to be more Christlike by knowing and claiming the righteousness of God *by the faith in Jesus*. Was I too bold? Was it unholy to have the idea that I become righteous like Jesus through his blood, the *cross*, and my salvation? How, as a human, did I dare to believe? Was I ever to partake in, to consider, or even to contemplate what part of my life connected through the life of Jesus? I dared to believe through his life. In my younger days this seemed too complex to believe, but I held onto these ideas in my heart as a teenager and believed God sees and knows all. Were my youthful thoughts too far out, or were these not preached or taught as I believed? I did not realize that believing *by the faith of Jesus*, believing through his words, and believing through his promises I had tapped through to the realm of God's unseen kingdom manifested to me as a believer. Further evolving meant understanding his teaching of the *cross* where the death of Jesus paid our sin debt in full once and for all.

We only *fall from grace* when we think we have to do some performance, work, deed, or act all by our self-effort. Please, you learn to rest through God. Let God be God. God is and has been working on our behalf for over 2,000 years. The *cross* was his finished work. It is done!

I have experienced manifestations through God's *grace*, *mercy*, and *favor*. These manifestations mean that I have been blessed to have received various and different words of knowledge through God. My *conscience is in line with* God's words and God's promises daily, rather than today's society and today's problems. Thinking about God's words and promises is my focus, not my cares, fears, or my worries. Focusing on God's words and God's promises takes the burdens of the world off my shoulders. Jesus is my answer. God is love. His love casts out all of my human fears.

As humans, we sometimes choose to keep our eyes on our problems rather than depend and focus our *conscience* and renewed mind on Jesus. Worry is our unbelief working at its very worst and lowest. But, on the contrary, depending and willingly handing over our cares and burdens to God each and every day is our belief at its very best! I am committed to continue focusing on and submitting all the cares and problems I am faced with to my ever-present helper, Jesus. We are never alone through this journey called life. I know I need Jesus and his help, so I surrender and ask humbly in prayer. There is no human pride involved. I give all of my cares, fears, and worries to Jesus, and I pray you will also. If we worry, fear, doubt, and so forth, are these sins against God? Think about it. Our focus is not on Jesus but on our self and our effort now. Our conscience hopes in the ethical and moral Biblical principles of holy God for mankind.

Our God is a mighty God who loves us. Do you desire to know our creator just as God desires to know you? From the very beginning, God has demonstrated his amazing love and power through the Bible. It is my *hope* that by reading my personal journey through life, God awakens *hardened hearts* and imparts the knowledge of Jesus's presence and his almighty wisdom. His wisdom is the start of understanding his ancient, mysterious, and supernatural ways as well. This knowledge is in the belief in the nonjudgmental love of God. As you believe in and love God in your very own special way, he will make himself known to you. You, too, will begin to experience God's *grace, mercy,* and *favor*. It takes a daily commitment in the renewing of your *conscience* as you go to God with childlike faith as you focus upon him as first place in your life.

Praise, thankfulness, and gratitude must be sincere and from your pure heart. I would not and could not go to Jesus otherwise, except with the intention of presenting my genuine heart. It is to honor Jesus who paid it all for mankind's sins. It has been done for you and me. I accept and claim God's love as a believer. This is how our faith in the unseen kingdom evolves. I release faith by speaking out loud about my faith. We are to be Christlike in all our words and actions and be witnesses to unbelievers. You believe in Jesus, you have faith in Jesus, you accept him, and you make him Lord of your life. This is the first step as a believer, allowing Jesus to take away all your sins within your *sinful nature* as a human and for you to partake with Jesus through his free and precious gift offered through his love and righteousness.

The calling and purpose of this book is for this Granny to offer what I have been freely given through Jesus. Why? This morning it was made clear through the *Spirit of God* that I extend this as Jesus's invitation to whoever reads or hears about this book. All of us have our choice to decide right now, so you should not wait until later. You, please, accept Jesus within your heart this moment. Do not delay. This book is written as a witness to *glorify* God and that his people will hear his voice and will see and know through this reading how important your salvation is to God. It is so simple. Why is it so hard for people to go to Jesus to ask him to be their Lord with childlike faith and a pure heart? Our shepherd watches over us. He is waiting for all of his children!

In the King James Version of the New Testament, Romans 10:17 is read, "So then faith cometh by hearing, and hearing by the word of God." Romans 10:10 is read, "For with the heart man believeth unto righteousness; and with the mouth confession is made unto salvation."

You follow his teachings and live by his ways, so your life will be a blessing through God to others. When all who live turn and live by the will of God, there will be increased peace and righteousness, reverence, sacredness, mercy, prosperity, and blessings for every member of society. God's abundant storehouse overflows. Jesus is our supplier. God wants you to be a part of his family. Jesus gave his life for us. You accept his offer; you won't find a better answer your whole life. As Christians, we learn that we do not receive because we do not ask in the name of Jesus. It is not selfish to ask God to bless your family, your friends, and you every day. God's blessings give us an opportunity to bless others. Ask God for increases in your finances, health, and what you will ever need. By your faith in Jesus, you will begin to see manifestations in other areas of your life. A note about prosperity is that in today's world it means having money and being rich. To me, prosperity is to have Jesus who is the one who increases the knowledge of God within us as to who Jesus is in our world yesterday, today, and tomorrow. Jesus is my choice. What is yours?

Another process in the life-long journey between you and God is to cultivate and nurture a personal relationship with him. Enjoy the process and have fun getting to know him. Yes, this is the most serious step anyone takes in life. It is joyful and happy as much as it is serious. I remember the intense passion and determination I had to know Jesus. I had a strong desire to learn about him as I remembered him in the Bible stories I read as a child. I recall wondering what it would have been like to follow him around and to hear his teachings. What a delight it would have been to see his face and look into his eyes! One day I will. My *hope* and prayer is that you will have that opportunity too. So, I urge you to ask Jesus within your heart and work earnestly at building your very own relationship with him. Desire and seek him continually, and your life will be forever changed.

I offer this prayer to believers as a rededication and to unbelievers to recall and receive Jesus today. Words do not have to be elegant or lengthy but from your pure heart.

I pray, "Father, soften and open our *hardened hearts* toward you. We receive you as our Lord and Savior, and we are yours forever. *By the faith of Jesus*, we ask and do receive through the name of Jesus. Thank you, Lord. Amen."

God's people in this world today are hurting. Go to your *Heavenly* Father who created you through his life, his own breath, and who lives within you and me. To address Jesus as Abba Father, one of the holy names he's known by among other endearments mentioned in the Bible, may be a strange concept. I wanted to include this because many people growing up did not have or know an *earthly father* as a role model. A father may not have been present in a home or did not show any emotion such as saying words of praise to express how proud of you he was as his young son or daughter. You may not have known your biological father, or he left when you were a young child. A father might have remarried and chosen not to include his children from his first or previous marriages. There may have been emotional, mental, and physical abuse. A father may have been in jail or prison. A father may have had to travel or be on the road to have a job. An accident, a sickness, or death may have changed the relationship between a father and a child. You have the *One* who has been your true Father all along; you do know that Jesus already adopted all of us as his own forever. Whatever childhood you may have experienced, you will prevail through your *heavenly* God who is our *one* and true Father. Our *Heavenly* Father is for our heartbroken men, women, and children of today who want to be a *whole* person. Abba Father wants you to ask for what you need. He has an abundant storehouse, which is overflowing if you only believe it is available to you as a believer. Jesus is the answer to our human needs, which are willed to us through Jesus according to God's appointed and due time, not ours. Wait! Be patient! Rest in the Lord!

I pray, "Abba Father, I believe you hear my prayer for this specific need. Because I ask, teach me to be persistent but not repetitive in my asking by using the same phrases or words with doubt that comes with not believing. I believe. Thank you, Emanuel, Prince of Peace, Holy One, and Counselor. Amen."

Chapter One

Delight Yourself in the Lord

AS A YOUNG child, I was not aware I was already delighting in the Lord by thinking of Jesus in Biblical stories, caught in daydreams of what *heaven* would be like, hoping to hear from God personally, and believing Jesus is as real today as when he walked on the earth. I wasn't aware that I was delighting in the Lord by trusting he would guide me through each day of my life, walking every step with me, and wanting his thoughts and desires to be my thoughts and desires. I was not aware I was already delighting in the Lord by loving Jesus and believing he would deliver me from any evil or evil thoughts within my human sinful nature *if* and *when* I made a mistake, or what I refer to as *missing the mark*. I know I missed some targets dealing with situations and circumstances through life, so this phrase is important to me to know that we do miss the bull's-eyes, our aims, targets, or marks as humans. No matter what, get back up and try again and again. Do not give up because it is the trying that pleases God. All of these are ways to delight in the Lord. This is what Jesus desires from all of us.

When I delight in the Lord, I know who I am through Christ. I am a child of our living God. As a human, I am not perfect because I am flesh and bones, but Jesus's power is within me. His power is greater than anything else that might come before me. Knowing any transformation would come from and through

Jesus, desiring to go through whatever evolving process is needed to be perfected by Jesus, delighting myself in learning how to truly worship Jesus, and coming before God in honest prayer was between just Jesus and me. Learning to talk to and to trust Jesus as my best friend, going before Jesus with *all my mess*, and being cleansed by Jesus is the process of loving him. Mostly, it is the knowing that Jesus loves me. My *missing the mark* within my internal thoughts and selfish efforts brought me to the point of asking to be cleansed of those misguided thoughts, performances, acts, and deeds. I was not even aware that by imagining laying my mental lists of human faults at the *cross*, releasing the control of my life as a human over to Jesus, and letting go of all old religious routines, religious rituals, and other religious doctrines were being taught by the *Master Teacher* through his Holy Spirit. Thanking Jesus for his love and his forgiveness and having gratitude that all my *missing the marks* are wiped clean is praise. Knowing I am saved through the blood of Jesus lets me experience Jesus releasing his power to my spirit. By me partaking through surrendering is in the holy knowledge of the power of the Trinity, which is the Father, the Son, and the Holy Ghost in one. Going to Jesus ready to receive his *grace* and his *mercy*, being blessed by God's *favor*, and being one through Christ is another way to submit with praise. When you delight in the Lord, you will experience and know God's love with *his peace and his love beyond human understanding* because of the name of Jesus and who Jesus is beyond measure. Amen.

We just have not been taught much about God's power given to us as well. Yes, it is God's supernatural might given through the *Spirit of God*. I mean no disrespect concerning sermons I heard preached over many years. I could not relate to some of what I heard about the "hell, fire, and brimstone" preaching. Our congregations are just beginning to hear the renewed message of God's love, power, and Holy Spirit. Let us hear it often and repeatedly. The people of God need to hear about his power through each of us as his witnesses and about our own shared and personal relationship through God. We are always presented with choosing between total opposites in life; will you choose Jesus or not? Will you seek and talk out loud to Jesus and about Jesus or not? Will you witness and speak to other people about our Beloved who is the source of all our life? The entire Bible speaks of who Jesus is, who God is, and who the *Spirit of God* is in and through our life.

I love reading the Psalms, especially when I need to recall how David connected to God through his prayers. David humbled himself before God by seeking and believing in the power of God rather than sulk with too much pity. He sought God. Psalms is a good place to start in the Bible. In your normal tone of voice and with simple words, ask God to unlock the door and to renew your mind, your heart, your spirit, your soul, and your physical body as you read his words and his promises. Take a verse at a time. Renew your mind and your *conscience* of God's love for you. Close your eyes. What are God's words speaking to your inner spirit? Ponder and meditate upon what you read. His word is like a double-edged sword. You may read a verse again at another time and get a new or completely different message as you evolve and mature through Jesus. The Bible consists of history, parables, books inspired by the hand of God, love messages from God to us, moral standards and life lessons, his truth, his light, his promises, and so much more. Your evolving depends greatly upon your reading and understanding of the Bible. As a believer, I am evolving each day.

I still go to Genesis because I love to read about the creation of God's universe. I read the historical names, but I do not get discouraged about pronouncing them correctly or by recall. It is about the generations and history before us with God. Delight in reading about God and his ways. To be honest, there may be days that I may not be able to read the Bible. God is not mad at me if I do not read that particular day. It is my spirit that convicts me that I need to read daily about God, Jesus, and the Holy Spirit. Other days, I enjoy reading to the point that I do not want to stop reading my Bible.

Remember, in the Old Testament people did not know what *sin* was. They did not know they were *sinning*. You will read that they could not come before God with any animal or other sacrifice with any blemishes as part of their obedience. People had to bring a sacrifice before God each time for their atonement and to show their obedience. There were so many religious laws to live by back then. There were over six hundred laws, too many laws to remember, and too many to keep by any human. If one law was broken, it was as if all were broken. The Old Testament is hard for me to read at times because of the way people lived, especially with the brutality. God was so, so patient for a very long time with his people who forgot him. They were under the Old Covenant of the Law.

Thank God, we are under the New Covenant where *all sins* are all finished once and for all. It is done! Jesus paid that price in full on the *cross* through his blood. It is hard to comprehend for some people. I do accept and claim my salvation by holding Jesus in reverence before Almighty God. God loves me, and God loves you. God finished it at the *cross* through the blood of Jesus. I go to him feeling secure, safe, and confident, knowing I am not condemned. I am so *loved* through his unconditional love forever in God's eyes. I come to him as I am. God will clean me up, teach me his ways, and carry my loads of cares, fears, and worries. He clothes me with his protection, speaks through to my inner *spirit heart*, and digs deep within our *spirit heart* to reveal who he is. My mind will be renewed each day through his mind. My *spirit heart* will be renewed and whole through his heart. My soul will be renewed through his soul. Yes, my physical body will be renewed through his physical sacrifice on the *cross*. I am one with God. God is one with me. We are united as one; I knew that when I first believed in Jesus. We had already been forever connected through eternity; we just have not taught or believed that too often as his children.

I know when I am a human being of the flesh. It is a sense of feeling heavy, and I don't like being controlled or governed by the flesh, which are the thoughts and the *nature of sin* as a human. I know and sense peace and lightness when the *Spirit of God* overpowers the flesh because I am always immediately aware of God's power through me daily. God knows that I delight in him and ponder his greatness throughout each day. It may be quick prayers throughout the day, or it may be a long prayer another day. A prayer may be a silent whispered prayer or spoken out loud. Prayers, praising, thankfulness, and honestly honoring God by talking to God should be natural expressions of our daily love toward God. Honoring God may be being of service to another person whenever you see or hear of a need without being asked. It may be giving my time to help someone without boasting about what I did. It may be a song of praise that is sung on the spur of the moment. It may be looking into my three grandchildren's eyes with love and witnessing that love returned. I look for those moments to experience Christ's presence and to be Christlike. If I sense that I fail to respond as Jesus would have, I ask immediately for his prompting and correction to be more aware and able to respond with love more quickly the next time an opportunity comes my way. It is the *trying* and *motive* that God sees and knows. Self-effort is by you and you alone, so any action, act, deed, or performance where God is not the main focus or center is the meaning of *falling from grace,* which God teaches us. With each new day, God does extend his grace every second of that day. Remember and believe each day that we do not ever lose God's *grace.* Think of it this way: I go from *grace* to *grace* because it is God who covers my back so to speak. When we do fail, God does lift us up to make us stronger for the next test and trial. Do you think that is why we need to learn more about God's *grace* and to thank God for extending *grace* that we did not ever deserve in the first place? What I am is by the *grace* of God. Because Jesus came to serve mankind, let us make that deliberate and *conscience* mental effort daily to be of service to others through the love of Jesus. It is that kind of service God does bless because Jesus and you are now partners through servitude together. Shalom. Amen.

I believe that Jesus has a sense of humor.

Jesus might say, "Finally! 2015! My people are considering me and asking for my help! Where have they been?"

Chapter Two

In the Beginning

AS A CHILD, I grew up in a small town over fifty miles from Charlotte, North Carolina. Being raised a Southern Baptist, our family went to Sunday school, sat on the back pew to the right of the church almost every Sunday morning, and attended revivals. Belonging to the Girls' Auxiliary Group, singing in the choir, and participating in Sunday evening church dinners was typical of my upbringing. Our family and other family members shared afternoon lunch most Sundays together. Our family attended Friday night football games and other sports activities in our community as well.

At the age of around twelve or thirteen, I heard a sermon about the gifts of the Holy Spirit, and I prayed about wanting to know about the future because I was curious about what was to come. I remember praying that I did not want to be able to read minds because I thought that would be an invasion of privacy. God heard my prayer. It was around this time that I walked down the aisle, joined the church, and was baptized. Even outside of church, I wondered where God was after hearing the Sunday school stories of the Bible. Was God a fantasy or real, and could people have a personal relationship with God like Adam and Eve, Moses, and other people who God spoke to during their life or through their ministry? I wondered where God was because I did not feel God knew who I was as a young child at that age in my life, but I did believe that Jesus was alive in today's world through his word and his promises. From an early age, I inwardly began to seek God within me and knew Jesus would not be just one part of me; Jesus would make me *a whole person*. Jesus would dwell within me. I would or could not even consider the fact that Jesus sees my heart, mind, spirit, and soul as separate. We are Jesus's total package. In silent, prayerful meditation, as well as in spoken words with childlike faith, I asked Jesus to reveal himself to me somehow, some way, and some day. Even though I did not feel like a special person, I knew that I had been touched by God because of believing Jesus to be the Trinity: the Father, the Son, and the Holy Spirit. I had heard the Holy Spirit referred as the Holy Ghost also. However, I knew I was special in Jesus's eyes. It is my *hope* that you feel that you are special in God's eyes too.

During the summer of 2004, I found my individual 19″ x 15½ ″ black and white portrait my dad had a photographer take, which had been stored in my parents' attic during my adulthood. Our family portrait was taken at our home that Easter too. The picture of this gawky, teenage girl now hangs in my bedroom as a reminder of my years from a teenager to the present. Fond memories are of my grandfather handing out Chiclets gum to us when we became bored, fidgeted, or began to talk during the long sermons. I loved growing up in a small town much like the television show, *Mayberry*. In fact, my dad was a magistrate and was associated with the police department. Everyone knew and looked out for one another. Family, friends, and neighbors would set one another straight before getting into too much mischief.

While I was in the third grade, our family lost my two-year-old little brother due to pneumonia. I remember very little about him except him wearing my sister's or my navy pocketbook on his arm, with the pointed hat to match, and was walking in my mother's high-heel shoes as he wiped his nose with a tissue. One Saturday morning, my mother was holding down his tongue with a spoon due to convulsions. His picture is hung in my home. Looking back now, my mom and dad were never the same and hardly ever talked about our sibling. Toward the end of their lives we talked about their son and my brother. No one was to blame; it was his appointed and due time according to God's will. Why? That question will be answered one day in *heaven.* Experiencing death at a young age certainly helped me to accept death more easily for some reason. As a result, I took an interest in near-death experiences in the '70s because the stories gave insight into heaven.

My dad was diagnosed with terminal carcinoid colon cancer, which metastasized to his liver and eventually to his brain. He died at the age of seventy-three in 2004. Being a teacher allowed me to stay with my parents during the summers after school was out in mid-June. My father was not afraid to die but did not want the pain. In jest, we prayed that he would fall out of bed and slightly hit his head, so he would not remember too much. I called one afternoon in late May to hear my mom say that Dad had fallen out of bed and was talking crazy. I wondered why she had not called the ambulance. I knew this was the answer to the prayer Dad and I had prayed together. My husband and I took off for North Carolina, and I was able to talk, feed, and bathe him from that Tuesday until his death early Saturday morning during that Memorial Day weekend. To lose a parent, especially one's dad, is devastating. I know how much Dad loved God, and Dad had told me that he was ready to die when called to *heaven.* It is my *hope* that parents and children talk about death, their beliefs, and God in order to give peace to one another before dying. I miss Dad every day. No matter whether a death is through cancer that is prolonged or a sudden death like a heart attack, there is no closure. One is only to manage each day the best way possible. One may go through the routines of each day because one may have no other choice but to carry on as usual. There may be a day when all of a sudden you feel as though you have awakened from a dream-like state. You just made it through a test or a trial through Jesus. A prolonged death may allow time for the ill person to receive love from others, and the caregivers and others involved are able to receive what they need for whatever reason God sees fit to do so for his purpose.

There are so many memories that I hold dear when I think about my dad. For some reason, my older brother and I seem to recall fondly us getting wet as we got into Dad's large walk-in shower to help him bathe. I would put on my bathing suit, but my brother would get in spontaneously while dressed. Dad needed help because he was as large as John Wayne. None of us were too embarrassed to help with his daily living necessities. It was an honor to do this for someone we loved.

Nine days later, on June 7th, our mother died of a massive heart attack at the age of seventy-six. She had broken her hip about a year before and had broken it again earlier that next January. She was getting along as well as expected, but I kept thinking that six months is a timetable I had heard about for an elderly person's chance of survival. The second broken hip during a short period of time concerned me. She was physically worn out taking care of my dad. She was stubborn and wanted to do it herself as much as possible. We had talked by telephone that Sunday afternoon, and she had mentioned having a little indigestion. As I look back, it was her "good-bye" conversation because she was thanking me for helping with Dad. I told her that what I did for Dad, I did for her also. It brings tears to my eyes as I recall what words were exchanged between mother and daughter. We then received an unexpected phone call a little before midnight about Mom having a heart attack. Our bags were quickly packed somehow. My husband was stopped by the highway patrol at least four times. Luckily, they believed him when he told them we had to get to Charlotte, but we did not make it in time. My older brother had been at the hospital and called us within several hours of completing the seven-hour trip with the heartbreaking news. My husband pulled over to the side of the road in a dark, vacant shopping center, and we both cried. In shock, I felt like an orphan, but I knew God was my *Heavenly* Father. My parents had been on loan from God on this *earth*. Because of the faith of each of my parents, I was able to feel God and their love and peace beyond understanding. My mom had also said that she was ready to die when called to *heaven*. When I look at losing someone so suddenly, I know God has a purpose in that way of death too. Personally, through sudden death it seems that the person does not need to linger to receive from anyone for some reason, and others do not need to give. It is the *giving* of people and *receiving* of people during pending death, and the people who are around at that person's death that intrigues me.

Since then, my older brother and I talked about being raised Baptist and the sermons about hell, fire, and damnation that we heard growing up all those years. In the midst of losing both parents in 2004, we talked about our belief in a loving God. One realizes that some people are better off than you are in life. With God's *grace* and *mercy* you also realize that you are better off than most people. Trials and tests are part of life; it is the way you respond that counts. As God grows me up, I choose to respond with a thankful heart.

<u>Here is a personal note</u>: I attended various church services to earn a Girl Scout badge. I would consider myself to be nondenominational as I continue to visit other churches even now. My heart remains with the church in my hometown to this day. I will repeat the message that we are one through Christ. Our personal relationship with God is vital in life. These messages need to be repeated to sink deep within our *hearts* that *God loves us*.

My faith would be tested and deepened. In 2000, my husband's face was red, so I asked that he get his blood pressure checked. He said that his face was red due to working in the summer sun and working during the wind-blown winter months. He started coughing up blood and was then diagnosed with lung cancer. He had one-fourth of his lower, left lobe removed. He never smoked. He and the doctor were against a whole-body scan at my request to check if cancer was anywhere else in his body even at my out-of-pocket expense if not covered by his insurance. Later, I will tell about my husband's terminal carcinoid liver cancer that was already at stage four before the discovery of the lung cancer. This was so similar to my dad's cancer. My husband often said that if my dad could deal with cancer all those years and at his age, then he could too! I often think of my dad as being an inspiration to my husband.

Again, I wanted to tell you about life's tests and trials before I told you about words of knowledge. From my journal over forty-plus years ago, I wrote about some of my words of knowledge prior to this book and had given some of my family and friends an incomplete copy of this manuscript as a book in binder form as a Christmas gift in 2011. Whether any family members or friends believe or remain skeptical, that is up to them. My reason for writing this book is to share my life experiences with my sons, daughter-in-law, grandsons, siblings, and friends before I die. I would never lie about any experiences; I may just change the locations, personal medical conditions or situations, and etc. to protect an individual.

As a young girl, I wondered if I might marry or not. I wondered what my future husband might look like. I wondered if I would have children or not and what they might look like. I did not seem to want a big wedding for some reason. Something private was my way of thinking. I thought about going to college and marrying around the age of thirty. I did not know if or when God would direct what my profession would be in life. My life was in God's hands.

I am grateful for my Christian grandparents, parents, and the church family I grew up knowing. Family has always been important to me. Another person I greatly admire is Reverend Billy Graham. I have never met him even though he lives close to Charlotte. Reverend Billy Graham is an inspiration through God for my generation in the '60s and for today. Thank you!

Here are the words of knowledge I was blessed to have received in various ways. Remember, there is no owner's manual that comes with this gift. As I experienced each at a particular time, I look back now in thankfulness and gratitude at these words of knowledge from over the years and see what a blessed journey I've had and will have through God. I sought, believed, and prayed it possible through prayer through God. It is for you as well. The words of knowledge are not necessarily in order but relate to stories and particular events. Certain words and phrases will be repeated in other chapters just in case a reader flips through any one chapter and not other chapters. It may be my only chance to grab your attention to what the entire book is about, so you do not miss out on the important messages as you skim through a few pages.

In early January 1972, I met my future husband. He reminded me so much of my father. I was not ready to get married in my early twenties. When he first called, I did not accept his phone calls because although we liked being together I felt like I needed to study rather than date too often. I had a knowing that he was the one when I had heard his name for the first time. By May, I heard the inner voice say, "Take care of him." I obeyed that knowing. Our wedding date is May 22, 1972, and we were married nearly thirty-nine years.

As another school year began after Labor Day in September 2000, my husband's biopsy indicated immediate surgery was needed. While in the hospital and waiting during my husband's lung surgery, I felt like I was handling the circumstance well on my own with his sister and a few friends that periodically dropped by during their free time or lunch. There was a couple that stayed a while. Because of my inner pride, all of a sudden I felt overwhelmed, like the rug had been pulled from under me. I felt chaos as in despair, anxiety, and turmoil in a way that I had not felt moments previously. It was during that time I heard the same inner voice say, "It is I who lift you up more than you will ever know." When we think that we are the ones that have the strength to handle anything, I am here to tell you that it is God who supplies that strength every moment. I am reminded that God sees and knows our life struggles, and I am the first to ask God for help with small and large needs.

I *hope* you will be interested to read about my words of knowledge. God is not a genie, a fairytale, or nonexistent. You will find him, and he will find you. As I experienced God more and more and in nature, I tried to keep my human heart, mind, spirit, soul, and body as pure as humanly possible. God made his presence known to me. I kept my whole heart, mind, spirit, soul, and body focused toward God. I am very human, so do not think I am perfect. I am far from being perfect! All of this did not happen overnight for me. Who am I to say that it might happen suddenly to you? That is up to God concerning your life. The journey is worth it! As I said in the beginning, I would like to share my experiences and blessings with others. In turn, *I hope* more people feel very comfortable in sharing their own personal experiences because I sense there are others who have experienced as much or more than I have. We need to be able to come forth and let the world know about God's blessings.

God bless the small towns across the United States. My heart belongs to the state of North Carolina and to the home of my birth. In my small-town church where I was raised, as a teenager I asked Jesus to make himself known to me. I received because

I asked. Jesus did make himself known to me. Blessings and answers to prayers manifest when we say prayers to God.

I will take this time to tell you why I chose this title, and I will summarize the book in chapter twenty-four. This book is called *The Answer* because Jesus is the answer. Jesus is the *only* answer. The name of Jesus is truth, light, love, and the answer needed by all today. Remember Jesus. Read his holy words and his holy promises. Be in awe when you witness his words and his promises fulfilled. As a Christian, I am not as amazed or taken by surprise as I was when younger or even with age now because through Jesus I know, believe, and expect to see his wonders daily. *All* things are possible through Jesus. As a Christian, I am in daily *fellowship* with Jesus through prayerful meditation. I am in a personal partnership with Jesus. I am not talking about a religion with Jesus; I am talking about my *spiritual intimacy* through Jesus as a Christian. As believers and as Christians, we should fall in love with Jesus. As we learn to submit ourselves to Jesus every moment of each day, we evolve to be like Jesus. It is a work in progress throughout each moment we live. Read your Bible daily about his words and his promises, so you stay connected to the *Spirit of God*. Talk to Jesus in prayerful meditation. Pray to Jesus who is our Father in *heaven*. Jesus loves you. Jesus loves me. He is not mad at you or me. Jesus wants unity in our love together. Jesus wants the bond of our peace together. Jesus wants to be your *all* and my *all*. Consider Jesus daily. He is waiting now. Jesus is the answer. This book is written to *glorify* Jesus, God, and the Holy Spirit. *By the faith of Jesus*, Jesus is the one and only one who obeyed God. It is Jesus's obedience to God that we are his beloved children. Shalom. Amen.

I will write about evil in a chapter called "Evil in God's World," but I wanted to include comments about our society in this chapter as well. Jesus is the only answer as we hear and read about greed, selfishness, entitlements, lies, fraud, deceptions, scams, and other numerous and various corruptions that could be added to this list. I will acknowledge here and now that Jesus is the answer to every problem our world will ever face. I believe in God's supernatural and *spiritual* unseen world. When we live by depending upon our own self-effort, we have *hardened hearts* toward God. Jesus wants us to depend upon him, not on our own self-effort. God wants his best for all of us. Yes, Jesus loves every one of us beyond human measure. I will address the *spirits of evil* in that chapter. Let us pray for our enemies, as Jesus required.

It is not selfish to pray for yourself, so pray, "Father, bless me today. Keep me safe throughout this day. Keep me safe as I am on the road running these errands. In the name of Jesus, keep my car in good running order, please. Thank you. Shalom. Amen."

Address whatever daily need to Jesus. Recognizing and thanking Jesus for all his blessings will lead us to gratitude. Heartfelt gratitude opens the door for you to witness his increase for even bigger blessings to come. How we relate to each free gift through *grace* and how we respond is seen and known in God's *heavenly* kingdom. Creation is one example that comes to mind as I revere nature. Be thankful for the rain; everything needs water.

"Jesus, how great thou art!" I say in response to the rain and watering of his creation.

The *Master Teacher* has taught me to stop complaining, especially during prayer.

An example would be, "Oh, God! My feet ache again today!"

I now stop and think during prayer, "Thank you, God, that I do have two feet to walk upon!"

I will try not to gripe to God. I will turn my complaint into a prayer of thanks and gratitude. All this moaning and groaning closes the door for Jesus to activate his blessings and for manifestations to flow upon me. Manifestations are blessings that flow through God because of God's *grace* and because of God's *mercy* and not through my self-effort. My heart has become hardened when I ponder the problem or situation and don't rely only on Jesus. I am learning daily to hand over my cares, fears, and worries to Jesus. Mentally, the load of my burdens does lay at the feet of Jesus where I have automatically placed them. That is where I find my rest, joy, and peace beyond understanding. Why? I am tired of trying to handle any worry by myself. I wondered why I did not feel real joy. What was missing? Jesus's strength is my joy! My real joy had been robbed from me all those years when I, all by myself, focused on the cares, fears, and worries of the world. My mind still held onto the cares, fears, and worries even when I knew within my heart that I unburdened them by means of the cross. I tried to rationalize by thinking of who, what, where, when, why, and how Jesus was going to solve each and every circumstance for me. It was not my faith that cancelled out Jesus supplying my needs. It was my unbelief and my self-effort! Jesus has given innate faith within you and me. I did have faith and did not need more faith; I asked Jesus to teach me about unbelief. We either trust Jesus to keep his words and his promises, or we chose not to believe in the words and promises of Jesus. The strength of Jesus has given us the answer. The answer is this: As believers, by the faith of Jesus, we are to ask Jesus through prayer to let Jesus know and then believe that his answer by supply is already on the way. It is done! It was done over 2,000 years ago. My blessing for any need is on the way. God's supply is in abundance from his *heavenly* storehouse where there is no shortage. There is increase beyond our human comprehension. You have *not* because you do not ask Jesus.

Recalling the name of Jesus, pondering upon the words and promises of Jesus, prayerfully meditating on who Jesus is and what Jesus has done, and talking to Jesus in prayerful meditation leads to spiritual blessings and for all of our *heavenly* gifts to be manifested. Manifestations are these free gifts from Jesus that do begin to show up as what we know or consider to be coincidences, what we know or consider to be miracles, and what we know or consider to be answers to our prayers. One of the greatest free gifts from Jesus is to know I am indeed loved unconditionally by the Father, the Son, and the Holy Spirit. *I* know: there is no doubt.

I use the word "I" because that pronoun is profound when one knows how precious and loved I am by God. The usage of "I" is no longer a selfish, self-centered word. The word "I" is power for believers in Jesus through the Father, Son, and Holy Spirit. That power is God's innate love that bridges our human spirits to know the *Spirit of God* within us.

As humans, we may choose to ignore the real truth of the power and authority in the name of Jesus. Even more so today, people believe it is impossible to hope in Jesus. So many have *hardened their hearts* to the fact that it is we, and we alone, who think we are in control and not Jesus. Society has turned away from the truth of who Jesus is yesterday, today, and tomorrow. I do believe, trust, and have faith, love, and know *all* answers are made known by Jesus Christ to his believers. Jesus wants all of his people to know him, his truth, and his love. The answer and truth is that all of us need to choose to renew our minds daily to who Jesus is to us as people in the world God created. God will renew our hearts, our minds, our spirits, our souls, and our bodies daily as we yearn for Jesus. That personal relationship enlightens us to our self-worth and to the empowerment of who *I am* in the knowledge of knowing God within me. *I am* through and within Christ; Christ is through and within you and me. The *Spirit of God* is our *Master Teacher*. The Holy Spirit is real and lives within you and lives within me.

Biblical stories and characters are so prevalent in our Christian teachings, especially stories about Moses and the Ten Commandments. This was the Old Covenant of the Law as described in the Old Testament. As a human being, I know there is no way to be perfect and to keep all of the Ten Commandments. Even as a child, I wondered who could. We all try to be Christlike, hopefully. In each trying, I was aware that to try as a human was to keep my heart, mind, spirit, and soul focused on Jesus, the Son of our living God. I craved to have a personal relationship and to know God. The craving went deep within my being to my internal and spirit heart. My spirit was awakened to faith, belief, trust, hope, and love within and through me that wanted to connect through God eternally. During deliberate, quiet moments of prayerful meditation, I dreamed of what it would be like to hear from God, from the *Spirit of God*. During certain days, I wondered and prayed that God would honor my prayers of thankfulness and gratitude for all the blessings offered according to his will.

Grace is a free gift from God that may not be worked for, earned, or performed. To me, *grace* is evident when you know Jesus's love manifests what I need at his given and perfect moment in time. Another free gift from God is *mercy*. To me, *mercy* is evident when you know and witness the loving kindness that Jesus extends to us humans each and every new day. With each new morning, a new chance is offered to recall Jesus who shares his creations with us through his love. Another free gift is *favor*. I do want the *favor* of Jesus to be upon me. To me, *favor* does manifest as the answer from Jesus. Jesus is the answer, our supplier, and our abundance; Jesus is our prosperity. Jesus is the answer for each of our decisions and our choices of every minute of each day of the week and not just on Sundays. Because of the *grace, mercy*, and *favor* of Jesus, I am covered under that umbrella through Jesus. There is no other person, place, or thing I surrender to daily but to Jesus. I am not giving up my life to Jesus; Jesus gave me life through and within him as the Son of God.

Because of the *cross*, we are under the New Covenant. Our sins are forgiven as believers. Yes, we may *miss the mark*, but we are forgiven. Because we are forgiven, I would never want to intentionally grieve or hurt the heart of God. In prayer, I pray that the *Spirit of God* teaches me, guides me, and opens his windows and doors concerning his plans for my life by directing my daily walk with Jesus through Jesus. I am no longer under the laws of the Old Covenant, thank God. Jesus loved you and me so much that he paid it all. His blood covers our sins. It is so hard for human beings, as mortals, to accept this free and loving gift. Why? Jesus breathed his breath of life into us. With Jesus, through Jesus, every breath we breathe means we are one. We are all one in Christ. I am one through Jesus. This will be taught *collectively and through our conscience* to each of us through the Holy Spirit concerning our ethical and moral principles. The Holy Spirit is our own individual teacher for our own path for his will for us, the *Master Teacher*. It has always been at the heart of my prayers that God pour out his Spirit upon the United States and world soon. We need God in today's world. I, for one, do *love* Jesus. Do you? Do you believe in Jesus or not? As a believer, you will not be embarrassed to say the name of Jesus. If you truly want to know Jesus, you will obtain all your answers through the Father, the Son, and the Holy Spirit. Shalom. Amen.

<u>A personal note</u>: As we see the world events unfold concerning wars, kidnapping and killing of children, disasters in nature, the spread of Ebola and the possibility of other diseases, and many other things, we are to be as solid as a rock in our belief in who Jesus is to you and to me. We do see with our

physical eyes, but we need to believe in the words and promises of God through our *spiritual eyes* no matter what we see or hear on the daily news. Yes, each of us is born with the innate faith of God within us. Yes, the scientific field of study needs to hear this. Our minds must not be divided in our belief in Jesus nor our hearts be divided in our belief in Jesus. Any kind of mental disbelief or *spiritual* disbelief will be our daily challenge to face as believers. Jesus is with us. In the midst of world events, Jesus must be your rock of foundation. With Jesus, through Jesus, every breath you and I breathe, we are one. We are all one in Christ.

Chapter Three

There is No Earthly Learner's Manual

I WAS ABOUT to learn more about the *knowing* from God. When my two sons were young, I helped my mother-in-law's neighbor deliver magazines. I would earn about forty dollars, which would buy a week's worth of groceries in the late '70s. While dropping off a magazine, I backed out of a business driveway in a small shopping center and drove into a deep ditch. The sign in front of the business had a towing sign posted on the outside wall. The location was across from the Colony on 17th Street and Virginia Beach Boulevard where a paper supply store had been in business. I was on the side street that went through to the Convention Center at that time.

I remember whispering to myself, "Well, there goes all the money I made today!"

All of a sudden, while I was deciding what to do, a beige, four-door station wagon drove near and stopped. Four, muscular, African-American men got out of the car, never said anything or even looked at me, picked up the car out of the ditch, got back in the station wagon, and drove away. It took me years to even mention this to my husband or friends. It took years to realize that I had been visited by angels that helped as soon as that heartfelt prayer had been said. To me, I learned God hears our whispers, our silent prayers from the heart, and the ones we just talk to him honestly, sincerely, and with thankfulness.

It was a simple, childlike statement heard by God quickly in a time of need. It became more evident and believable to me as a Christian that God sees and hears it *all*. God hears even our inner and outward heartfelt comments. God was within me, and I was with God. It became an intimate love for God. God watches over us, and God cares about you and me.

I have seen prayers answered immediately, other prayers may take years, and some may be days or weeks. Some prayers may not be answered according to our terms or will. It was my prayer that my husband be healed of cancer. A lesson was that it be God's will, not mine. Some days, before my husband's death, I still asked in prayer why the cancer had no cure.

Several years later, I heard the inner voice say, "I am that I am." I began to try to accept, understand, and know that my husband was on loan to me while he lived on this *earth* as a gift from God. A lesson that I learned lately is that I did pray with belief that God would heal my husband. I did pray for God to help with my *unbelief* when I was not able to believe. Help me with my unbelief. I will mention about recently hearing a soldier from a church in Atlanta, Georgia speak. He mentioned that God has to *break ground* to do his work. Before anything is able to be constructed, there is ground that is broken. With my husband's death, God *broke new ground*. With the suffering of my loss, God is using me to *break new ground* through him. I finally got my answer from this soldier who had been in war. Thank you for sharing your message, so I have no *unbelief* concerning accepting my husband's death. I know my husband is safe and with God through God's appointed time of death. One day, I will ask God why my husband was not healed. I believe this book is what God has called me to write. We are to *glorify* God, and by sharing this book you will acknowledge the Father, the Son, and the Holy Spirit in your life as well.

There is more about angels. Angels are, but not necessarily, like what we read about in the Bible. They may be multi-racial and come in the form we are able to accept or need in a certain situation. Later, a friend would tell me that an African-American angel visited him when he was gravely ill while in the hospital. We shared our stories. I believe we are here to be of service to others; we are *earthly* angels.

My husband and I went to a friend's house for a party in the mid '80s. During the surprise party for our friend, I sensed that his house was in the process of being robbed as we were celebrating his birthday not too far from his home. I had seen an episode of *Unsolved Mysteries*, a popular show on television at the time, which had shown a person who had sensed the same as me, reported a robbery, and was jailed. A teenager in the neighborhood had been spotted coming out of our friend's house around that time and was caught by the police soon during our party.

I mentioned what I sensed to my husband, and he said, "Oh, you are crazy!"

I did not know what to do. First, I could not go alone to check it out. Second, our friends could go but would possibly get in the middle of the robbery. Third, I could call the police. Eventually, the suspect was caught and known by a few of us. My husband remained a skeptic about me knowing things ahead of time. This was the first premonition I had about a crime occurring. The inner knowledge was becoming advanced to the point where I would need to think before I handled any situation like this because I had no experience.

In the late 1980s, after finishing a college class one late afternoon, I was driving home from the university. As I got on the interstate, I sensed that I needed to go slow and stay in the left lane, and the sensation was strong. People were mad as I remained in the left lane, some cursed, and others displayed finger gestures as others blew their horns. I kept going slowly. Suddenly, a young girl swerved sideways and hit the cement median. Had it been a different driver, her driver side would have been hit broadside. I was able to stop. She was able to back up in heavy traffic and straighten her car in the right direction. I thanked God that I listened to the sense I felt and thanked God that the girl's life was spared. I was blessed to have had a hand in God's work with God that day.

It was November 29, 2011, and I was turning the television channels and happened to come across a dedication to Randy Travis, the country music singer, at the Opry, the Tennessee country music auditorium. My uncle always kidded me about him because he lived less than thirty miles from my hometown.

One favorite song of mine is "Forever and Forever." It tells about growing old together. As I listened to the program, Randy Travis sang that song. I sensed my husband's love with me that evening. I cried and cried. Yet, I felt the same sense of peace beyond understanding and love. The love was of God and my husband. My husband and I talked about being together again in *heaven*. I mention this almost six months after my husband's death because I sense his love around me. There were times when I went into the grocery store and did not think I would be able to finish my shopping because a particular song we listened to was being played. I still feel this way today at times. The same happens when I automatically turn to another radio station, and I hear another favorite song of ours. I have learned to pay attention to these details because I am certain these are not just coincidences. At end of June 9, 2013, I was at the grocery store and again felt my husband's presence with me as a Josh Groban song played. It was "To Where You Are."

In the mid 1990s, when I was teaching a story in school that involved Native Americans, I sensed more about nature than I had felt before that reading. The story was about a painted desert, that happened to stir something within me. When I was younger, I liked the old cowboy-western shows on television. I liked learning about the Native American customs, especially the reverence and sacredness of animals, life, and nature. The importance of nature seemed to *electrify* senses within me. I began to hone in on everything as being of God, which I had felt always, but now it was also realizing that every single blade of grass was God's creation. I looked at all the different materials supplied and provided by God and what man has made. It is important to cherish all the elements of a product and what materials are given as a result of God's handiwork. All things and all people are to be respected with reverence. For me, nature initially opened the door to hearing through God in a more profound way. From there, doors were opened to learn more and more through the *Master Teacher* that God treasures nature.

In those earlier days, I felt the need to have private time for prayerful meditation. I needed that time to spend alone with God. You may want to read and reread the chapter "My Prayerful Meditation" and the chapter "Mind, Spirit, Heart, Soul, and Body." Now, I come to my conscience level that I explain as tapping into the universe's energy. I have not forgotten or discarded the breathing exercise, but I do not need or use it on a regular basis unless I feel the need to get to a deeper level than where I am at that moment. There is an *electrical* charge, or maybe the connection to God's love is the only way I am able to describe this in human words. I sense within my body that it connects somehow to the field of energy and love of our world. I try to pay attention to the *electrical* or loving vibes I sense because something is about to happen or knowledge is about to be given in a manner that I may have to figure out if it is not in the very familiar inner knowing, such as a mental vision or hearing precise *spiritual* words mentally. Later, I will give premonitions that were given with specific wording. I would never change the wording I have been given in any incident. It is the knowing and words heard through the *Spirit of God*.

These are my laymen terms that describe what happened to this wife of almost thirty-nine years and who became a widow at age fifty-nine. My husband was a skeptic for many years. My sons, daughter-in-law, and three grandsons may be skeptics to the end as well. I only want to share what I have experienced as their mother, mother-in-law, and grandmother. I believe and know that we are able to connect with God everywhere and daily.

God is within us, especially with the pure and honest desires of each heart, mind, spirit, soul, and body as we truly search from within ourselves. There are *conscience* levels revealed to us as we seek God that are within and through us. I know that I have tapped into the *Spirit of God* within me and through me. I am in reverence of who I am in Christ. This is a holy and sacred place I share through and with God. God shares that holy and sacred place within and through me.

Meditating is now done while on my feet too. If I am in line at a store, I am able to go to that holy and sacred place for whatever length of time I need to spend with God. I look for those chances to be silent and still during routine errands. These are the cherished moments daily I make as a *conscious* effort to verbally acknowledge whom God is with words spoken out loud or in silent prayers throughout each day. Prayerful meditating is scary for some people who think it is New Age or a Western culture idea. We honor God when we *consciously* think about him. It is a time to give *all* your worries to God. First thing in the morning as your eyes open, talk with God about your day. Thank him. Give him your gratitude. Get personal with God. God wants that personal relationship with you and me.

When you read the chapter "My Prayerful Medication," I will explain that I always envision a white light around me from the start of my prayerful meditation to the end. It is like having a lit candle circling me, which resembles an encased bubble dome in my *conscience*. This is the armor of God's protection. I am as one with the creator of the universe. God's protection is forever present. I acknowledge his protection where only God and his love surround me. From the place of love, I sense what I need to connect through at that particular moment in time and space. God's love stretches out, and I tap into another dimension through me and through to God's love. I do not know what happens exactly; I am just able to tell about my own personal meditation, which I know has led me to know God through his love for me. I am *consciously* mindful of the Father, the Son, and the Holy Spirit. The Trinity is not separate from me. The Trinity is the mighty power I know.

Chapter Four

The Knowing: The *Spirit of God*

EVERYONE HAS A sense of intuition, a gut feeling, or an extrasensory perception if one listens to God's inner voice. There is no learner's manual that comes with this. Take time, be quiet, and listen to what you pray and meditate about throughout the day. I have read the Bible numerous times. The first time, I wanted to relate to the history and events. The second time, I paid attention to the words Jesus spoke and events that took place with him. The third time, I read to know the man, Jesus, and his love for mankind. I am reading the Bible for the fourth time for my comfort and to rest in his love and peace. Now, I read God's words and promises because I trust him more than man on a daily basis. Yes, I write, highlight, and use ink pens to write in my Bible to the point where I am now on my third Bible.

In the 1970s, when in our early twenties, my husband and I were driving around just looking at houses that were for sale while our two sons were with their grandmother. I sensed that a dog had bitten the boys. I asked my husband to head to his mother's house right away. Sure enough, a neighbor's dog had bitten both of them. Animal control was called, and the dog had to be quarantined. Luckliy, the bites were not serious. I told my husband that the knowledge was given to me. I just knew it had happened.

It does not always work the same way each time. I would have to learn to listen to the inner *spiritual* voice. When I say it is an inner voice, one may think I am crazy. The inner *spiritual* voice that I know is one I have to tune into very carefully. With it I may feel an *electrical* charge throughout my body or a warm, peaceful, and loving knowing is felt from my head to my toes. I know that one is not to totally go based on what one *senses*. I will call it an *electrical* charge of love. So when I do mention it is what I sensed, it is the *spiritual* inner voice. It is the *knowing*.

This happened over the years. A word of knowledge I once received concerned a friend driving late at night to a second job after working a day job. It was my maternal instinct to ask a friend to be careful. So far, nothing had happened. However, I was told that the family almost had an accident when leaving a celebration my husband and I had attended sometime within the last ten years. Falling asleep while driving seemed to be what I sensed about the friend being alone as he was going to his second job and back home. I will take into account that the family was safe and an accident was avoided not on his drive to and from a second job but leaving a shared get-together. I was recently told this after voicing my earlier concern.

It was a maternal feeling rather than a premonition. Another account happened when a friend opened a new business. Again, my maternal instinct kicked in because I wanted to make sure the friend had the fire insurance policy. Nothing happened, and I took a chance to voice my concern anyway. Later, I will write about a restaurant burning that I had sensed as another early premonition, but I had little experience on how to handle such knowledge without possibly being a suspect or accused in any crime.

I went back to night school for years and graduated in 1989. I sensed I would need to have a degree to be able to take care of my sons and myself in the future. In 2000, I heard a loud whistle sound one time as my husband slept during the night. I thought it might be lung cancer. Throughout this book, I will write about my husband's terminal carcinoid liver to lung to brain cancer. At first, he ignored my requests to go to his family doctor for another chest X-ray since his work X-ray had been negative months beforehand. It was then that I realized I could only do so much when another person may choose not to listen. It was a valuable lesson to learn because I often asked myself how far am I to push someone to listen, when do I back off, and are there times I am to remain silent? People make their own choices and choose not to listen to reason. All the pleading to my husband and to the doctor for a full-body scan landed on deaf ears. I was about fifty years of age when I lost my parents. I felt like an orphan. My sons were in their thirties when their dad died. What a blessing to have had my parents twenty more years! I knew that Mom would not be able to go to the hospital when the time came for Dad to die. She wanted his funeral service at the funeral home because she knew that she would not be able to go back to church if the service was held there.

May and June 2004 are very painful for me to write about still. Dad died Memorial Day weekend. As I sat across from Mom after Dad's funeral, I sensed that she would not be living long, maybe a week or two. I wondered if I should tell my brothers, sister, or my mom what I sensed. Would she want to know? How do you tell someone, or do you? I looked at a woman who had lost her husband and knew she would not want to live without him. He was seventy-three, and she was seventy-six. I knew she was going home soon and knew she loved God. We lost our mom nine days later due to a massive heart attack. Now, I am able to use a sense of humor with a comment of what my dad might have said to Mom in *heaven.*

Dad would say something like this, "I leave, so who's watching the children?"

I miss them every day and wish I could pick up the telephone to talk about what's going on and hear their voices. Love and respect your parents and grandparents. Don't take them for granted! We talked about God and *heaven* during the summers I spent in North Carolina. I did ask both of them to watch over my family with love and protection through God.

When I came home after Mom's service, I went to a local restaurant with a brother who stayed with me the rest of the summer. A man walked in that looked like our dad. I gasped and did not mention the man to my brother because I was not sure how he might react. We had seen the newly released movie *The Notebook,* and I had wanted to cry out loud at the end of the movie because the movie hit a raw nerve for me about losing both parents several months previously. They probably would have called the police if I had gotten so hysterical. I did cry out loud all the way home. The movie holds a special place in my heart to this day.

"The Mighty Oak" is a poem I wrote as I sensed the strength nature demonstrates to us.

Writing this poem flowed so easily and quickly as a young adult.

When I need a living thing on Earth to inspire me,
By your mere presence, you have given me that
strength I need.
Nature gave you as a source of persistence and endurance
and love,
My heart's content when I thank God for such a source
from above.
Where would I be if I couldn't look to you for inner peace
and content?
Nature has provided such earthly treasures for each and
everyone due to God's sentiment.
Your inspiration lives within my soul, inner spirit, and heart.
This person can stand tall, firm, in my own commitment and
not depart.
This is because you stand erect and true.
I have inner fortitude, and that's the message I've attained
from you.

Chapter Five

Evolving as a Seasoned Christian

AT THE TIME each event happened, I was learning through God. Now, that I look back at the accumulation of all the events, I see that they were blessings! Being a sensitive person definitely helps one to stay in tune to everyday circumstances and to learn through God and life. Whenever I feel heaviness, darkness, or prolonged sadness, I pay attention because something is about to happen. The darkness is like a dark cloud that lingers over me or in my mind until the event occurs. Over the years, I have tried not to watch too much news because my knowing tends to be dulled otherwise. I may think of an individual for a while, so I know that is a clue that something is about to happen. Thinking about someone or something may be immediate, last a few days to two weeks, or around a month and more.

I loved the Beatles as a teenager. I still have the *Double Fantasy* album. When I saw the black and white album cover, it seemed like death to me. I sensed it before John Lennon's death. The date was December 9, 1980, and I had never experienced anything like that before concerning a well-known musician loved by so many people. I continue to get that same experience whenever I handle the music cover.

Weeks before June 12, 1994, I thought it strange to be thinking of O.J. Simpson. I knew who O.J. Simpson was in sports, and I liked the Hertz rental car commercials, especially with his mom in the airport. I knew him as a Heisman Trophy winner and wondered why he lingered on my mind. This was probably one of the first words of knowledge about a well-known personality that I received with unexplained sadness. Then, within a two-week time span, he was on trial for the alleged murder of his ex-wife and her friend. At this time, I think it best not to comment further. Forgive me. That is a year I choose not to think about too often.

The *knowing* may or may not be about well-known people or situations. With each *knowing,* the experience may lead to different outcomes. My husband and I were at our favorite restaurant, and a younger friend close to our sons' ages worked there. One evening as he had stopped to talk to us, I sensed that he was not well. I did not know what his illness was or how bad, but I needed to make sure his insurance and other paperwork had been completed since he had not been working there too long. I made a fuss, and my husband was annoyed with me at the time. Later, we found out that the paperwork had not been completed, and our friend needed a lung transplant immediately. Much later, our friend and I had the chance to talk about why I was so persistent about him signing the paperwork that evening. After his surgery, we had the chance to talk about angels. Our friend mentioned that an African-American angel had come to him in the hospital. I told him about my car-in-the-ditch experience. We spoke of *spiritual* things before his early death.

Was I ready for outcomes that may be of a natural, suspicious, or criminal nature in the early 2000s? I had been in a store near my local shopping center, and as I walked out I sensed that the restaurant beside the store I just left would not be there much longer. In my mind I thought of a kitchen fire, possibly arson, and tried to think of other possible reasons to explain what I was sensing. This sensation was immediate. I thought about going to talk to the manager. If someone asked for my name, would I be questioned and jailed later? This experience happened very early in my life. At times, I am still reluctant about how to handle these types of situations. The restaurant burned within a two-week time period. I do not recall what the reason was when I read about it in the newspaper. The reason I was reluctant to act concerning this early experience was that a man had been put in prison who had the same gift and had reported the possible arson or burning of a building. I had seen it on the television show called *Unsolved Mysteries* where police questioned how he would know this information if he was not involved.

This sensation happened again in the early 2000s. I had visited a friend at their place of work. It was late on a Friday afternoon. As we were leaving, it was the first time that I had ever sensed a place of work not being there come Monday. I thought I was going crazy! I talked to the friend's boss that I knew, and the subject of extrasensory perception, or ESP, was presented because of what I had sensed before leaving. The person acknowledged that ESP is real, but it was hard to accept when everyone just wanted to go home and didn't want to take the time to listen to me. That very early devastating experience has always stayed with me because of arson.

I am learning and on my own, except through God. I wanted my husband to support me, but I realized that he could not fully understand. It has been lonely over the last forty years. I have trusted a few friends to tell what I have experienced. This is probably why other people with the word of knowledge gift do not speak out more. At times, it is very rewarding and personal. On the other hand, I have been unable to share with all family members. I want them to know the experiences of my life. They may not believe what I write here. I am writing the truth of my relationship through the creator of the universe. In earnest prayers over a span of time, I asked for an even closer personal relationship through God and for him to give me a sign that he heard my specific prayers of concern. Those prayers were not prayers of doubt or to test God. It took many years before I saw my personal sign from God. God is so patient!

Originally, I asked for birds to be sent, specifically orioles because of their orange color. Later, I could not tell the difference between an oriole and a robin, so I asked for cardinals, the state bird of Virginia, as the sign. The birds come when I'm in prayer and have come unexpectedly from God, which comforts me. I needed them so much twenty years ago. Now, they are still a blessing to me from God. God knows the desires of one's heart, mind, spirit, soul, and body. I hungered to know God and have the special bond between God and me. I am able to sense that the cardinal or cardinals will come; it may be the next day, two weeks, or immediately. I know the sound they make. God sends them spontaneously from time to time.

In 2000, I asked that one cardinal come and sit and stay on the fence or tree a while. It did. The first cardinal is comfort and peace that I know how much God loves me and listens to my prayers. It was an important connection that I saw in the physical world because I had faith to believe he would show me the sign from his unseen kingdom.

When my husband and I decided to downsize when he was sick, he had found a house that had just gone on the market that morning as he drove in a certain neighborhood. He gave a contract payment right then while I was in North Carolina taking care of my dad. I came home long enough for the weekend and was not thinking of moving. I needed to go look at the house because of the contract agreement. On the way to look at the house, I was praying silently to myself because I did not know whether to sign the contract or not. I asked God to send me a cardinal on the property if I was to sign the contract. As we walked through the back gate, a cardinal flew overhead. God was part of my decision-making process.

A second cardinal came after the first cardinal had sat and stayed on the fence or tree a while. The second cardinal was a very personal prayer request. When this prayer is answered, I know that God will be in the center of it all and with all concerned. It is a wonder to see if it will be a female or male bird or both. Some are young, some are the elderly, stately type, and sometimes I see a combination of the mature, beautiful, red birds of Virginia.

The third and final cardinal came after the first and second cardinals sat and stayed on the fence or tree a while. I have sensed a *spiritual awakening* of the *conscience* happening in our world. I want to be part of that, don't you? I do not know what part I will play, and I want my sons and grandsons to know that they are why I have been a prayer warrior for our nation and world as a wife, mother, and grandmother. Is this the breaking of ground for all of us through God as we are reminded to recall and to speak the name of Jesus in today's world?

Months after my husband's death, I was asked to get away for the weekend with a relative and her husband. It was a secluded, rural area surrounded by nature. Upon waking early the next morning, as I was getting ready, the relative mentioned seeing cardinals. I had told her about the cardinals the night before as we talked. They stayed near the house over the weekend. What a comfort to see them when the birds had not been seen there previously! God was with me that peaceful weekend when I needed his love.

There are no coincidences. I was driving back home from running some errands and was thinking about my husband. As I stopped at the stoplight, the car in front of me was side by side with a car with the license plate MILU. I thought it was strange to see a license plate with only four letters or numbers on it. I looked at it again. All of a sudden, it seemed to read directly as "My Lou," in reference to me, as my interpretation. To me, it seemed to be a *heavenly* message and one of comfort when I was thinking of my husband and missed him so much and was feeling grief at that very moment.

Chapter Six

We Are Not in Control

WHEN I COULD not be with my dad after the summer months due to teaching, I was about to receive an important blessing. I was feeling like I was letting my parents down because I wanted and needed to be in North Carolina to take care of them. On the way to school, I thought about my parents daily. I thought about God's word and his promises. Was I going to trust God to take care of my parents or not? On the human level, I was not ready to let go and give him that control. I realized that I never had that control in the first place. It was all in God's hands. Everything!

When that school year started in the late 1990s, the sensation I felt had been building within me for a while. I pulled onto the main street heading west where the sun rose behind me in the east. The sun flickered, as if to get my attention. It was a brilliant orange glow of life. As I believed with less doubt, had deeper faith, learned to trust, and loved God more to take care of my parents, I began to see a rainbow ladder. It was straight up with the colors of pink, gold, and green. The colors are hard to describe; I would not do it justice. The rainbow ladder was with me for years on my trip to work. It was a blessing to show me how much God values his word and promises to us. The care of my parents was always in his hands, not mine.

My mom had broken her hip for the first time in 2003, and

I stayed in North Carolina longer than expected one summer night rather than going to a wedding my husband and I had looked forward to attending in Virginia. I usually went to bed close to ten o'clock most evenings and was tired. I was in the hall and saw a bright light coming from the upstairs bedroom where I slept. I should have been scared, but I was not. I got in bed to go to sleep. I saw pink clouds all over the bedroom ceiling. From the pink clouds, I saw string-like streams of mist coming from the clouds. The mist covered the entire room. All I felt was love. I sensed that God wanted me to feel his love because I had done the right thing by staying with my parents when God knew how much the wedding meant to me. If I had not experienced that myself, I doubt that I would believe anyone telling me the story about them experiencing the same. I had *sensed something* coming my way!

God speaks to us in many ways, gives us our own personal experiences and expresses his love in unique means, and I have learned to be open to what I sense from God. I do say that I accept it if it comes from God only. I offer thanks and praise to the Father, Son, and Holy Spirit. I may read several different books of the Bible in one sitting one day. The next day, I ponder the words of God and hold them dear within me. When I wake up in the morning, God is on my heart, as well as during the day and at bedtime. God is within my heart, mind, spirit, soul, and body each day. I am in constant prayer throughout the day. It may be a simple prayer while standing at the kitchen sink. If I am running errands and hear an ambulance, police car, emergency vehicle, or fire truck, I offer a prayer to heal the injured and direct the healing hands of all involved from the start to the end of their service.

I have learned to say, "Thank you, God," in all circumstances as a way to express thankfulness toward God.

After my husband's death in 2011, I still say, "Father, you are my husband now. Protect me, and keep me safe throughout this day."

Each day, I sense God's power, his teachings, his comfort, his love, and his peace beyond human understanding. No person, no possession, or anything else is able to do what God will do, does do, and wants to do for us as his children. All we have to do is ask with a pure heart. You are not capable; so do not try to fool God. He already knows our intentions and motivations.

I was in my early twenties in 1972, and I went to the beach often around 8:00 in the morning. For some time, I sensed something from the sun, but I did not know what. It was then that I saw the pulsating sun. It meant life's energy to me. From the pulsating, I saw light pink around the inside of the sun, which turned a darker pink with time. I did see a light grayish or silver color on the outside of the sun that later turned darker gray or silver. I still see it from time to time, especially when I am thinking of God's wonders and of his world. To me, this may have been an earlier sign given about the pulsating energy of God's love.

I will mention my interests in science here and in later chapters. As this manuscript is being written, another word of knowledge has been given because I have asked within my being how I am able to tap into this knowledge through God. I know about atoms, which are comprised of matter and energy. Atoms make up all the physical laws of God's universe and the forces that are comprised in God's universe. Because God created his world, God is in control of its functions, its interactions, and its dependencies that are infinite in number. Everything existed at its exact moment. Because I believed that life exists in God's universe and was created by design, God's words of knowledge expanded because of my faith in God as our creator. I do love nature as well. I feel so close to God when I garden or do other work in the yard. This is why I use the word "sensation" because when I think of God, I think of nature too. When I think of nature, I automatically think of God. To me, God and nature should not be separated when it comes to the study of science. Think of the missed discoveries in science, medicine, and other fields of research because men and women have not connected God as vital in this work. When is mankind going to realize the power of prayer when trying to solve theories or cure health issues and just find answers through Jesus? Jesus has the answers to all questions concerning mankind. I do pray there will be a time when scientists and other experts learn that through prayer comes wisdom. What if these experts prayed together at their meetings, conferences, and with their patients?

God was about to show me that he was with me ahead of trials and tests. He knew that I would need him more than ever upon my parents' illnesses and deaths and my husband's illness and death. What I experienced is not what one might expect to experience in this modern time. God tailor makes his personal experiences for us to what we know and are able to accept. God continued and continues to show his love to me and to anyone who is open to his words and his promises.

From the sun, I continued to feel the sensation I know so well. I have been blessed to see the silver cord that is attached to us from birth throughout life since the 1990s. Again, I do not have words to adequately describe this silver that is like flowing ribbon. It looks fragile but is powerful. It glistens with majesty. It holds blessings of life. It is attached from the sun, and I see it on sunny days. It follows me when in the car and appears close toward the hood of my car. The silver cord is mentioned in the Bible in Ecclesiastes 12:6. What a blessing from God to see this!

That same silver cord was seen in December 2011 as I was sitting on the couch with the shutters open. The silver cord was stretching from the sun in my direction. Over the years, I had seen the silver stream inching its way from the sun in segments. Then, it slowly withdraws. I sense that God has been showing me that he is with me on the road and in my everyday walk in life. Here is another science lesson I have witnessed. From any beam of light, I see light that is in a straight line. If I am watching television or burning a candle, I see the light coming toward me in a straight line or as straight lines in different directions. It is a little science lesson I had not remembered or seen before but was taught as a child. I see this at night from the streetlights when I am driving, so driving at times is distracting. Recently, I have seen the blue color of light above drivers in their cars. It is amazing to see the color as I pass by cars and to see who has the color above their heads or not. I will have to investigate this further.

My newspaper had not been delivered one morning or the next. On the first morning, I sensed that something special was to happen. The second morning while driving to get the paper, it happened. It was close to the days before my husband died in January 2011. All of a sudden, I could not see anything but the sun. It was different than being blinded by the sun. I felt like I was having an experience like Saul when he was renamed Paul on the road to Damascus in the Bible. I could not see anything but a brilliant, golden light. I slowed down from the speed limit of thirty-five miles per hour to a snail pace.

I was talking to God in a humorous way saying, "Gee, I can't see! Don't you think it is dangerous when I can't see! I know you're trying to tell me my husband is dying. I know it is soon!"

I stopped the car because it was lasting awhile, and I did not know if I might hit parked cars or hit anything coming my way. This is an experience I will never forget! I knew that God was preparing me for my husband's death, which was drawing near. I know that is why I experienced what I did from God. Again, I am not sure whether I would tend to believe this encounter if someone told me about it if I had not experienced this *holy* moment with God. I was in the presence of God, and he made his love known to me when I needed him so much.

Because of his presence and who he is, there are moments during the day that I say inwardly or out loud, "My sweet, Lord."

That is who he is to me.

Chapter Seven

The Shemitah is Taught

MY MASTER TEACHER has been teaching me about the Shemitah, and I did not know during 2001 that I was about to be part of the Jewish and ancient mystery. The Shemitah is an ancient mystery, which began when the people of Israel turned away from God and the Ten Commandments at Mt. Sinai with Moses. In our modern time, I will only go back to 1973 when we experienced The World Trade Tower, the Vietnam War, and abortions in the United States. In 1987, there was a stock market crash, so I want Christians and nonbelievers to think of every seven years: 1973, 1980, 1987, 1994, 2001, 2008, and what about the year 2015? The Shemitah is the release, fall, collapse, or shaking up of our economy through recession, depression, Wall Street, our cities, our nation, our buildings, and more. The Tower Mystery is called Migdal, which is much like the Tower of Babylon in the Bible. We need to be aware of higher buildings being built in the United States for this reason. The Elut 29 is the last day of the Biblical calendar where every seven years God's people will receive a blessing and rest from God, or we will receive a curse and judgment from God. I am a Protestant, and the love for Israel was placed within my heart as a child. I am again blessed to be part of this word of knowledge. In 1917, there was the Balfour Declaration where the land given back to Israel was nullified. In 1967, Jerusalem was restored.

From 1917 to 1967 to 2015 will be the forty-nine years of the Shemitah to Jubilee. This is why I have been a prayer warrior for our nation too. I ask in prayer that the people of the United States remember and speak the name of Jesus. I want the world to have God's blessing and not any curse in 2015.

In 2001, I saw economic difficulties in big, bold black letters in my mind prior to 9/11. I asked my husband where he thought the hub of economics was located. I was thinking Wall Street or the New York Stock Exchange. He mentioned the World Trade Center during our conversation, which rang more true to me. I just knew there were economic experts handling these issues. Men are not in charge of economics, God is. God is in the midst of any and all circumstances in the physical world we see. In God's unseen kingdom, God is watching us and trying to teach our *conscience* to be of service to one another, to *consciously* love one another, and to *consciously* reach out to one another.

I will never forget September 11, 2001. The emergency number 9-1-1 was given. Around the end of late April to mid-May, the emergency number of 9-1-1 was being sensed. I kept wondering why the emergency number stayed with me so strongly. After much thought, I played around with dates. Later, the date of September 11th came to mind. It was like putting pieces of a puzzle together bit by bit. Information was unfolding as I put the last piece together, like receiving information from a human description such as an electrical energy or vibrating frequency. I felt the electrical energy charge from within stronger than ever. During this time, my family was planning our oldest son's wedding for mid-August. We all were busy. For the first time, I felt overwhelmed with the school year coming to a close, the wedding, and sensing this information over various months. By mid-to-late June, I sensed the Pentagon might be hit, but by what? I thought I was going crazy because this could not happen in the United States. Again, I just knew there were experts handling national security issues. I sensed that the Twin Towers might be hit but by when, late June to early July? Who do you call? Who would believe a call from a citizen with this information? Would I be taken seriously? I did not sense any information concerning the White House or Pennsylvania. Mid-July to late August, I sensed the time frame would be as early as

6-7:00 a.m. and would be completed around 10:00 a.m. I sensed the Boston area. I sensed that Alan Jackson, the country singer, was to write a spiritual song for all of us, so I knew that 9/11 was going to happen.

I was not feeling well during August and September due to a chronic illness. During that time, I questioned what I was sensing. As a human, it was hard to comprehend, even after all God had given to me. When in school, I heard that 9/11 was happening. I went to the ladies' restroom, got down on my knees, and asked God to forgive me for not trusting, not believing, and not loving him as I should have. My chronic illness in late August and early September had delayed me from pursuing different avenues to take. I know God was in the midst of 9/11, and that's all I need to know right now. It is hard for me to write this because I am addressing the age-old question we all ask. Why? I do not understand why God does not interfere concerning our roadblocks or stumbling blocks that happen. I have to acknowledge that man's gift from God of free will is each person's choice whether to choose to be a blessing or choose to be used as a curse against mankind. We will have all the answers to such questions revealed to us one day! Evolving continues and further knowing is explained in the chapter titled "Evil in God's World."

Over the years, I realized I was receiving two messages at once. The messages were about our economics and 9/11. I have reached out to agencies since and was told that I did not have enough specific or detailed information for anything to be done. I know there are other people who sensed this kind of knowledge through God. With bits and pieces of all our information, would there have been all the evidence to stop 9/11? There is not a day that goes by that I do not think of 9/11.

How do I know that God is in the midst of every circumstance? Like everyone else, 9/11 changed us all forever. The *Spirit of God* inspired me to write the "Women of the World in Prayer" after 9/11. It was written in less than twenty to twenty-five minutes. I *hope* you are inspired to be a prayer warrior for our world, our children, and our grandchildren. I am including this prayer because it was given to me through the hand of God. Let us keep our eyes upon Jesus. Let us keep our eyes upon our *Heavenly*

Father. Let us keep our hearts focused and open to the *Spirit of God*. Amen.

In 2014, I went back to read the prayer to see how far I have evolved through God. I have to add that Reba McEntire, a country singer, was on my mind before she wrote her new song called "Pray for Peace." The theme of peace had been on my mind constantly, and I hummed those words. I am not a good singer, so when I heard Reba sing that song with that tune I knew it was a gift from God. She does acknowledge that as well. What a beautiful song with the Scottish bagpipes given to our world for today. Thank you, God, and Reba. Amen.

I will include this prayer as it was given after September 11, 2001, for our world.

The "Women of the World in Prayer" is a prayer I was inspired to write, believing that great-grandmothers, grandmothers, mothers, stepmothers, mothers-in-law, sisters, sisters-in-law, daughters, daughters-in-law, aunts, nieces, other relatives, and friends will be united in our faith to change the world in which mankind lives today. As co-creators with the creator of the universe, the emotional, mental, and physical pains and burdens of our hearts are instantaneously received and heard through prayers. Please, share this prayer with the other women in your life. Here's to the men joining the spiritual journey together with us as each accepts what is believed at this moment and what resonates in each heart to be true.

We say, "I pray to the creator of the universe that each day may your light and love surround us. Guide and protect our families, friends, and other people we come in contact with daily. May we connect with you: mind to mind, heart to heart, soul to soul, and spirit to spirit. Remove fear and doubt, so negativity is replaced with God's love, mercy, grace, and compassion offered through the universe's energy. You are the force that holds the universe together. May we always keep our eyes upon you. As we pray for the president of the United States and the world leaders, descend your Holy Spirit upon all. Guide and protect our leaders, military personnel, and their families. May each leader and every citizen of every nation become more moral and wiser as you unveil your knowledge and wisdom, so senseless acts of violence are not tolerated because we sense the sacredness and reverence of life and of nature. This day, as we pray, we humbly ask each home to be blessed, so every person is given a second awakening to have a more open heart. Bless us by deepening our belief and faith in you as our friend, our heavenly Father. Knowledge, belief, and hope are our seeds of trust, so we believe and experience that you are as close as our next breath. This knowledge and your love's energy are the sources given to us, so we may love and take care of one another, serve one another, love unconditionally, and give forgiveness.

Our faith in you lets us feel assured that we are where we need to be presently. We sense that you are present in our physical world by the way you lift us up more than we will ever know. Your presence is in all things as we read your words, see the beauty of a flower, hear a newborn baby's cry, feel the sun's warmth, smell the ocean's breeze, taste the quenching water... your love expressed in many forms and beyond in the realm of the nonphysical world we believe to exist.

We pray, especially now, against evil in our world. We pray, that as we are tested individually while here on earth, that we call once more upon you and your help in every detail we are faced with daily. Let us remember not to place human characteristics on your omnipotent power. You know the earnest desires of our heart and the motivations behind each heart. By knowing this, believing this, and having faith in this we may ask for anything we need without ceasing. We pray against evil, destruction, and even terrorism. We pray that terrorism is disbanded, led to a state of confusion, and discovered before any harm comes to any people or country. Send your warring angels and your angels of principality to guard and protect us by air, land, and water.

As we pray together, speak your name more and more, seek you daily, remember to thank you for our blessings in blessed or personal trial, we extend a grateful heart to you.

Father, Son, and Holy Spirit extend your love to us. We will continue to ask specifically and in details for what we need. Thank you for hearing our prayers. Let us be your instruments of love as each soul evolves, so life is lived and perfected according to your will. Let it be...let it be according to your agreement with your master plan and us until we return home to be with you throughout eternity.

Let us remember and rejoice with childlike faith again in innocence how we once expressed with bowed heads, folded hands in prayer, and on bent knees before Almighty God. You alone know and personally understand our human faults and frailties. You laugh, cry, and still love us no matter where we are standing and no matter what the time. You are among us; you are always with us. Bless these women and men who pray and walk in faith with me this day. Amen and Amen."

Chapter Eight

Our *Collective Conscience* is to Love Jesus

GOD IS LOVE, or love is God? While in Vacation Bible School as a child, that question was asked of the class. I pondered that question periodically over the years. God is within us. God knows when we have the burning desire to know who he is in our life. God is not just the church building. The heart knows and reveals his truth. Pretend you have a key that unlocks your heart. Take the key and open your heart with his pure love. Tell the Father, Son, and Holy Spirit that you want to be filled with belief, trust, faith, and love that he is only able to give with his *grace* and *mercy*. Remember, one must want God with so much desire. Do the same with the key to your mind, heart, spirit, soul, and body. Read his words, and hold his words and his promises within your heart's desire. I still have that desire each day. The *Spirit of God* knows me better than I will ever know myself. God will seep that desire to know him within your heart through his love, his knowledge, and his cleansing. You will begin to see who he is to you personally.

I already mentioned attending different churches as a Girl Scout to earn a badge or two and enjoyed going to the different churches. I felt we are all God's children. Why are there so many various denominations? My opinion has changed somewhat over the years because God does treasure diversity! In the Bible, Jesus was among many diverse groups of people and cared for all. We need to share our *spiritual* experiences with others because we will be able to tell others who God truly is to us as an individual, that God is very much alive today and real in today's world.

I was inspired by the *Spirit of God* to write the Senators and House of Representatives and to send the "Women of the World in Prayer" several years ago. The only response from a few was to contact my Virginia representative on the matter. I would like to say that I am not affiliated with any one particular religious denomination at this time. I was raised Baptist, but my choice is nondenominational because I feel comfortable to go to any church and not be restricted by doctrines imposed by any churches. I am not affiliated with any one political party. Today, it is hard to vote for a candidate due to moral issues. Voters pick the best candidate with what information they have among the different candidates. Because we do *not* seem to be able to forgive any candidate's *nature of sin*, we are losing intelligent personnel when we are to still love God's child. It is my prayer that we learn to separate the difference when it comes to judgment.

I think of our forefathers often. They spoke of *providence*. I believe their decisions were based on following *providence* in everyday life and moral decisions that affected them. *Providence* is evident in their writings, historic documents, and their faith. These men and women were not perfect. No one is perfect. The phrase "In God We Trust" was so evident in their lives. Our polls say that over 80% are Christians in our country. Why do we appear to be the minority? I believe in the separation of church and state. However, I do *not* believe that praying should have been taken out of our schools. When a nation takes God out of any equation, I believe evil *spiritual warfare* creates chaos by creating stumbling blocks, deception, trickery, and any means planned against our nation because we have chosen to forget God, to not hear God's words from the Bible, and to not see God's promises and blessings freely given to us. None of this would be done out of hate or meanness on God's part. We, as a people and as a nation, will be faced with the unseen and *evil spirits* ready to attack our minds, our hearts, our spirits, our souls, and our physical bodies! That is why I am repeating the fact that we need to renew our minds daily through Jesus.

I am pro-life and believe life is sacred and to be held in reverence. Abortion is between God and the person or persons involved. The comfort I receive is that all aborted babies are God's children and are with God in *heaven*. We love the people involved. It is God who is the only and final judge. You will read in the chapter "Evil in God's World" that unseen forces of evil spirits deceive, trick, are cunning, and use every plan to condemn, create negativity, and corrupt human minds every moment of every day. Our nation is suffering, and will suffer, the consequences of not seeing life as sacred and revered. This is not of God but the *spirits of evil* who want and do try to take dominion by invading our minds. As believers and nonbelievers, reading and knowing God's words and God's promises is so vital. *When* and *if* we as a nation do *not* realize these demonic forces, they will try to dominate and fool our way of thinking in our lives as these unseen forces corrode our society. I hear comments like our country has gone downhill, gone to hell in a hand basket, and other words where there is no *hope* but only despair in this world. That is why I repeat we need to renew our minds daily through Jesus, so we are ready to guard against evil forces.

Our nation was founded upon knowing and believing in God. Our nation needs to turn back to God where he is our God, and we are his people once again. We can love anyone who *misses the mark*, just not the *sinful act of nature*. Let God be the judge of any person. We would never be the first to cast the first stone in that judgment of others. We are all guilty of placing ourselves above other people when we think we are better, smarter, puffed up with a prideful ego, look down on any class of people, say that we would never do whatever that person did in comparison to what we think, and ponder any and all evil thoughts within our minds. You never know what God's plan is for another person or why and for what purpose any given situation or circumstance happens. But God knows.

Why is marriage described as the kind of institution that implies marriage is bad these days? God created men and women for the holy purpose of marriage; marriage is still to be between one man and one woman always and forever. Amen.

God was in the midst of our marriage. In January 2011, I sensed God was going to answer me in some response to my most personal prayers. If not to heal my husband from cancer and have him live, I was about to witness God's *grace* and *mercy* according to God's love and will. Upon learning of my husband's cancer and during prayers, I knew God was ministering to my husband. I wanted to know and see the hand of God upon my husband's life. I knew I might not know or hear all that God was ministering to my husband during his sleep, dreams, or his increasing coma-like sleep. About a week before my husband died, my heartfelt prayer again to God was to know or hear my husband say that he surrendered it *all* to God.

While nearby in another room, while my husband was sleeping periodically one evening, he called my name in a loud voice and said, "Lou, I surrender it all to God!"

It is my belief that God is ministering to believers and nonbelievers, even as death approaches. Why? God does not want any of his people, his sheep, to be lost. It is during our sleep, dreams, and holy-moment encounters with God that God is watching over us whether we remember it or not. I do not fear death. It is my most cherished wish to *go home* to God at his due time. I am ready!

My prayers continued to be answered. A few days later, I heard my husband talking in the middle of the night.

My husband was talking to Mother Mary saying, "But, Mary, if I have to go that means I will be without her the rest of my life."

I was raised a Protestant, so praying to Mother Mary would be a strange concept. In my own personal relationship to God, I had been praying many years to God that he would allow his mother to attend to my husband when his suffering was to be too much to bear. I wanted Jesus's mother to take care of my husband. Mary had seen and known suffering. I wanted her to be with my husband because it was a desire of my heart as my husband was about to die. God heard me.

I say as I still ponder heavenly love during prayers, "Thank you, Mother Mary, for hearing and answering my prayers. You spoke directly to my husband that night, Mother of Jesus, you whom the Wise Men kneeled before to honor your son. It is you who stands near your son in *heaven*. It is you who is close to God and the throne room in *heaven*. Thank you for taking care of my husband for me. Thank you, Father, Son, and Holy Spirit for Mother Mary and her love. Amen."

A few days before he died, my husband said, "Because I have not complained, I am being lifted up by the saints."

God is love. I was blessed to have been able to hear what I needed to hear because of God's many blessings upon me. Upon my husband's death, I grieved. I still do, and I sense God and my husband's love and peace beyond understanding. My husband seemed peaceful after learning of the already advanced liver cancer in 2004. He took me in our bathroom and pointed to the floor. He asked if I saw anything. He said that I could see it better if I sat on the toilet seat. I saw what he saw. We both saw the face of Jesus as pictured as the Shroud of Turin. I still see it today.

I asked, "What do you say it is?"

He replied, "The face of Jesus. I saw it weeks ago but wanted to keep it to myself a while."

I kidded him by saying, "The God who sits on the throne in *heaven* will meet you anywhere, anytime, any place, and even on your own throne."

We laughed.

A friend of ours was diagnosed with cancer during the time my husband was diagnosed. We would see our friend at one of the cancer locations periodically. One evening our friend called and wanted to talk about *heaven,* and the two of us took turns handing the phone back and forth to each other. We kept the conversation full of laughter. The important lesson we talked about was whether we could and would love God on the cloudy days as we love God on the sunny days? It had been a prayer of mine that I would be able to talk to our friend about *heaven* and that my husband would be present to hear what I had to say.

That friend's December prayer was given to me December 10, 2010. As I walked out the door that early December morning on my way to school around 6:30 a.m., the *Spirit of God* pulled me back inside to grab a card. I knew whom the prayer was to be for in my heart. The prayer spoke of God's arms surrounding our friend with his love. It was specific about being cured of cancer or not according to God's will, not ours. I had the privilege of being asked to read the Christmas Prayer as part of our friend's eulogy in July. I knew the prayer was to be heard by many before it was even written. I had sent cards to our friend. I knew which one our friend would choose for me to read because God inspired it for our friend. Now, that I look back, the prayer was for my husband and me, as well.

Prayers continued to be answered. After my husband died on January 9, 2011, I tried to get to sleep around 2:30 in the morning. Right before dozing off, I saw grayish spider-like fingers moving in front of my face. Then, I saw a yellow circle in front of a blue triangle shape. Both seemed to be enclosed in a dark, purple, vacuum-shaped ribbed hose. I do not know whether this was the tunnel, but I prayed about it because I wanted to know that my husband had gone through the tunnel we read so much about concerning going to *heaven*; I believe that is what I was allowed to witness. It is a blessing for me that God allowed me to see and hear upon my husband's death.

Our *collective conscience* is to love Jesus, and that is what it is all about in today's world. Amen.

Chapter Nine

Would You Want to Know?

THE KENNEDY CHILDREN hold a special place in the hearts of the American people. I heard, "He will not reach his thirty-ninth birthday!" I knew who he was. I was depressed upon sensing J.F. Kennedy Jr.'s impending death. No other information was given.

I also heard, "She will no longer be of royalty." I knew who she was. My husband and I were at a local restaurant and saw the news about Princess Diana's car crash. I knew she was not going to make it. Her two sons have always been on my mind because it was, and is, hard to see those two young men without their mother.

Duke University offered a psychic test at the Edgar Cayce Foundation many years ago while I was in the audience. I do not need to take a test or be tested to know what gift I have been given. I was not in the mood that evening to take the test, so I did not take it too seriously. My score was 80-85% just from goofing off during the test. I would not want to score 100%; that's God's job. In fact, this test was to name items on cards not seen. My gift is not like that.

Caregivers are very special people. I saw how my dad and husband thrashed around and sat up in bed toward the end of their life. It was an irritation like they could not get comfortable. My dad called out for his mother.

"Mama, come get me!" was my dad's final request.

In prayer, I would tell my grandmother to hurry and bring him home.

Toward the end, my husband asked, "Am I dying?"

My response was, "You are going home!"

Death is not to be feared. I believe humans are afraid of the way that they may die. I do not know if any family would even want to know about a loved one's impending death. Somehow, I chose not to tell my mom. The reason was because of what I sensed. I did not want to accept that word of knowledge because it was about my mom and concerning her death. Why would I want to cause her to worry needlessly? Isn't death God's final call?

David Bloom was the NBC correspondent I sensed was going to die as I saw him reporting during the war in Iraq. I did not know the cause would be a leg clot called an anabolism.

Peter Jennings was an ABC news anchor. As I watched the evening news, I sensed that he was ill for weeks before he made the announcement. I did not know the cause of his illness was lung cancer, even though I figured he smoked.

I sensed that Senator Edward Kennedy was ill as well. I did not know that the illness was brain cancer. I had sent an email to his office, which I do not know if he received or not.

A friend's grandbaby had been sick for a few years. I encouraged the friend to go home to be with the baby that day. I did not mention death from the common disease already known. I had been looking out a window previously and saw a yard full of orioles. Orioles were the birds I had first prayed to come as a sign from God. I changed my mind to ask for the cardinals instead because of the red color. When I saw the yard full of orioles, it grabbed my attention. I sensed the child's death was to be soon. The child died that weekend.

Another friend met with other friends and me. The friend looked ragged. I wondered whether the friend was going home or to do errands. She mentioned running errands and other work details she had to take care of before going home. I encouraged her to go home instead. She did not. Her husband died of a brain tumor before midnight that night.

A child's friend had been sick many years. As we met together with friends, I sensed pending death. Again, I encouraged my friend to leave to spend time with her loved one. Within days, the young adult died of a brain tumor. When death is sensed, it feels as if the person's life does not extend any further in this life on earth at that point.

My husband and I were out at a restaurant and a friend mentioned that his arm was sore. He thought it might be due to extensive exercise or running more miles than usual. I did not hear all of the conversation, but I thought it was symptoms of a heart attack. I got up early the next morning to go to the friend's house to drive the friend to the hospital. The telephone rang, and I told my husband before I picked up the telephone that it was the hospital calling about our friend. My husband looked so surprised. I asked him whether he believed in premonitions now. The friend survived.

Chapter Ten

Mental Visions

SITUATIONS AND CIRCUMSTANCES will be changed here to protect the persons involved. A young lady had gotten her license. She was with her parents in another state when my husband had mentioned the young lady was driving behind the wheel that weekend. I did not know what this mental vision meant at the time. This was another one of the earlier mental visions after envisioning *economic difficulties*. I saw a large "L" with a smaller "l" within the larger "L." Two weeks later, my husband mentioned that the young lady had been in a car accident at the corners of Lincoln Avenue and Lewis Avenue.

Years later, another young lady was going with an organization on a long trip out of the country along with her parents and other friends and their parents. My husband was going to be in the general area and would drop by to visit our friends. Earlier that morning, I had called and mentioned to my husband that he needed to check to make sure the young lady did not have a false identification card. I asked him to make sure he was around the group of young people to make sure that no one ordered alcohol. The parents were in the same hotel but in another part of the restaurant when the young lady was carded and caught. I wished I had called each parent separately while they were flying to their destination to tell them what I had sensed. They did not know of my gift then, but they do now. My husband wondered how I knew. I told him that I had been trying to tell him about such things for years. He remained skeptical to the end.

A word of knowledge may come while simply doing laundry, like it did one Saturday morning. I heard, "He will marry." I instantly knew whom the message was about at that moment. A friend of ours had been single for numerous years. My husband began to ask how I knew what I knew.

A college student visiting the beach area had been murdered, and I watched the news over the years as the trial unfolded. About a week before the body was found, I was given the name of a general location in another part of our state. I have not worked with law enforcement at any time. Luckily, the body was found in less than a week. I was given a general name, not an exact spot.

One spring, I was doing spring-cleaning for days. This was during my very early experiences. I had the strong sense to go to the large, public park at a close-by neighborhood. I was so dirty and did not want to stop cleaning. I did not pay attention to the sense. It was not a vision I saw. Days later, I read in the newspaper that a woman had had a medical condition and had died in her car. I went to the park that day and walked around to see the secluded area for myself. The woman's car was found at the very back of the park, so I am not sure whether I would have been drawn to walk in that direction the day I sensed the need to go there. This experience was the one that reinforced the need to obey God in the future and to stay in any area whether I wanted to go or not, or whether I was clean or dirty.

During Christmas time in 2004, while opening Christmas presents on Christmas Eve, Asia was suddenly on my mind. I stopped what I was doing and got a map of the area. It was a gushing sense of a great deal of water. It was the tsunami that hit the next morning.

I usually watch the evening news with Brian Williams, but I do watch other channels as well, and I noticed that the actor Michael Douglas was the new, introductory voice. I sensed some difficulty with his voice. It sounded fine, so I was not given any more than his voice would be silent awhile. Throat cancer was later revealed.

I had pictured a magazine rack and had wanted a metal one with a unique design. I had a color and certain price to stick to, or I would not buy it. I was amazed that I found the bluish-gray one for the exact price as I walked into a store within a day of going shopping. However, I had not thought of the sales tax.

Due to my husband and my back problems, I needed to buy a table with chairs to match that was higher up than our usual table. I walked into an antique store and saw what I had pictured in my mind. The table and chairs had just been brought in that day. The only catch was that another piece of furniture was part of the set.

God sends other people our way when needed. My husband walked in the door after work and acted like he needed to tell me something. He was acting strange, so I asked him whether what he needed to tell me was good or bad. He said that one coworker who had supplied his van had shook hands with him later that day because it was my husband's last day before his retirement. The coworker got to the gate of the business and turned around to come see my husband. The coworker had a prayer with my husband. I told my husband that God had sent him to have that prayer, especially for him. God bless you for listening to God and responding. There were Christians at his work, and I had *hoped* a believer would pray with my husband the day of his retirement.

God is concerned with all the details of our lives. He forgives us because we are human, especially when we feel or think that we do not measure up to him. No matter what the everyday circumstances, I know to keep my eyes upon him. No matter what trial or test one endures, it is your response to that trial or test that God entrusts to you. Some say that I did not have the right to be mad at God after my husband died. God knew that I would be, he knew for how long, and he knew the depth of that anger. After reading again the recent bestseller book titled *Heaven is for Real*, I was not mad. I had not been ready during my grief to accept that my husband was already in *heaven* and with God. In prayer and with thankfulness, I have acknowledged that to God. I had read many books about near-death experiences over the years but reading another book about *heaven* always seemed to take the anger away little by little when I could not let it go for months. I know a God that loves all of us unconditionally, and he is aware of us *missing the mark*, which is of our *sinful nature*. God extends his *grace*, *mercy*, and *favor* to believers in Christ.

God's given me this gift and these experiences. He knew that I would goof in many cases. With age, I look back to see how I was sometimes slow to respond correctly to what he was showing and teaching me. With age, it is still fun to be on this journey with God and to connect through to his love and forgiveness and patience. I learned to turn whatever problem or situation over to God in prayer. *All* is in his hands to control the outcome, not mine. That's a hard lesson to learn in life for any human who wants or feels the need to control everything. Turn it *all* over to Jesus. If one does that, they leave the consequences to God. Wait on him! Unburden now the load you want to carry alone. Rest! Now, God will go to work on our behalf. It is not our self-effort that brings the ultimate solution. Jesus is that answer.

Chapter Eleven

Passion and Love

I AM NOT a religious person, nor do I want to be called religious, but I would rather be thought of as *spiritual*. I do not know about all the religions of the world, nor do I know all of their doctrines. Our heart reveals what or whom we are passionate about in life. That passion is what we follow; I *hope*. In that passion, God reveals our mission and purpose in life. The love we feel is God's energy. Love, not fear or hate, is of God. Another hard lesson to learn is that we need to love ourselves in order to know and to willingly accept the love of God. Love awakens the heart to truth. Our lives will be awakened through that power, which is *holy* and the *divine spirit of God. Faith* grows like a small mustard seed. One becomes closer to God in thoughts, words, and unselfish deeds, and not by our self-efforts in life. Knowledge is the awakening of your *spiritual truths* when one accepts and listens to God's will with a pure heart. The economic difficulties may be the stumbling block from the *spirits of evil* in our world. God will turn any evil for good. Is God asking each of us to assess what is important in today's world? Have we become too selfish and too apathetic to the needs of others? Jesus's life was one of servitude; aren't we to be of service to one another as the children of God?

In the family we wagered a small bet on our favorite baseball team, and other family members joined in for fun. I sensed that I would win and knew the purpose for winning. I did not know that a neighbor needed the money. I handed the money to the neighbor as soon as I had won. I told the neighbor that I knew I was going to win it, and I knew that God had the neighbor in mind ahead of time. That morning the neighbor's oldest son had given the youngest son his last amount of money to pay the balance for a class the younger son needed to take one semester for college. The oldest son gave his brother his money, but he was not too happy to give it. The neighbor cried because of the situation and was glad to be able to give the oldest son his money back that same day. It was the same amount I had won.

Later, our family made another small bet with family members. I knew that I would win, and the same family needed the money. To be honest, I do not remember the reason. I obeyed God rather than keeping the earnings. I have not made any more bets since then.

When my husband was sick, I used all of my sick leave. The school system will allow employees to donate sick leave to another person. Over the years, I donated what was allowed to personnel who needed a sick day, even if I did not know them. There were two schools where I worked that donated time, so I could work one half of the day and be home with my husband from 12:00 p.m. to 1:00 p.m. each day for months until the next year when I knew that I would have to retire to take care of him. God provides when you give unselfishly to others in their time of need. I want to acknowledge these schools here and thank the teachers, again, who donated their sick or personal leave to me. God bless you.

We are all connected. When I feel like having a pity party, I go through my pantry and take what I have as extra to the nearest church pantry. When I do my spring-cleaning, I look through what I have not used for years and take it to a thrift store that helps with a local hospital or one that is associated with the care of disabilities. Again, I believe that God is giving us a chance to be of service to other people, which is why we are here in the first place. Our *free will* allows us to make choices to be his servants for God's service when God puts those choices before us on a daily basis.

Passion and compassion seem to be more evident in a person when that person has been through trials and tests in life. I was not going to read the "Women of the World in Prayer" at my husband's memorial. My youngest grandson walked into the kitchen in his pajamas with a pacifier in his mouth, looked up at me, and I knew that I had written it for all of our children and for all of our grandchildren. When my husband and I left the doctor's office in 2004 after learning of his liver cancer, he had tears streaming down his face. He was not worried about himself; he was worried about our children, our grandchildren, and me. He said that he would not be here to take care of us. He nudged in a loving way by saying that I would need to stay to take care of what he would not be here to take care of for too much longer, which was a reference to my mom dying nine days after my dad died. I saw a man that was thinking of and putting his family ahead of himself. My husband held the same values as in my prayer; only he would have used different vocabulary as a man. While he was near death, I quietly read the prayer out loud or silently to myself when near him as he slept.

When first diagnosed with cancer in 2000, I asked my husband," Why you? Why you of all people; you have a wife, children, and grandchildren. It does not seem fair when there are a lot of single friends. That is not right of me to even think or say. I shouldn't!"

My husband's response was, "Why not me? I would rather be the one to have the cancer, not you, not our two sons, and not our grandsons."

I have kept a journal of the words of knowledge I received from God over the last forty-plus years and recently gave copies to some of my family and friends in a binder book form one Christmas. Whether any believe or remain skeptical, that is up to them. My reason is to share these experiences with my sons, daughter-in-law, grandsons, siblings, and friends before I die. I would never lie about my experiences. However, in some instances I changed names and situations to protect the privacy of individuals involved. I look back now with thankfulness and gratitude at my blessed journey I've had over the years and will continue to have with God. I sought, believed, and prayed it possible through God. It is for you as well.

I wanted to share my personal journey with God while you are reading about the words of knowledge. I will let these words of knowledge or revelations speak for themselves. To me, there is *spiritual* energy within our universe, which is God's energy of love. God's connection is the only way I am able to use words to describe what I have experienced. As our *conscience* and heart levels deepen through God, we are able to connect *spiritually* through God. Think about what would happen should we all, as his people, *collectively and consciously* think of God at the same time concerning world peace, eliminating world hunger, stopping crimes and all natural and manmade disasters. God connects to the *conscience* levels and our heart levels we are presently at for our understanding and what we are able to presently accept. As we mature through Christ, that *conscience* level and heart level deepens and reaches a higher level and so does our connection through God *spiritually*. I was blessed to have connected through to the *spiritual* connection through God because I asked. Along with my *spirit heart*, my mind, my physical body, and my soul, I was ready and daily connected to the *Spirit of God*. Deep within my *spirit heart*, God connected through my heart and spirit. It is as if God looked within my heart and saw what I treasured; that is Jesus. This is my personal journey with God, and I *hope* and believe that anyone who reads this book will desire to seek God. You soak in even the smallest mustard seed amount of belief and faith daily in who God is, whether you are aware of it or not. Think of each breath you take; Jesus is through that breath that is your life. He is our life. I love God, and I love Jesus. I love the power and the authority of the Holy Spirit. The power I possess is the power and authority through God within me. God and that power are within you too. Amen.

When a cancer patient or a person with a terminal disease says, "Why not me?" with clarity, I know that God has already prepared that person to face the challenges in the days ahead. I recall that statement because I know the peace and strength God gave my husband. We talked very little about his cancer afterwards except about appointments, medical tests, and whatever he needed to do. God gave the two of us the strength to deal with cancer for ten-plus years.

"God is in charge of healing this cancer, not the doctors. We'll place our faith in God as we deal with your care," was my initial response to my husband as we got on with our everyday lives.

I kidded my husband by asking him to come up with some romantic saying between the two of us. It was years before he thought of doing that. Right before his death, he said that he had finally come up with something that was his best yet.

He was serious when he said, "You are the jumper cable that jump starts my heart each day!"

We both laughed because we both thought it was corny at the time. I kidded him that I knew it would have to do with cars or baseball. When I need a laugh, I remember his romantic gesture. The more I thought about it, this gesture of love was real after nearly thirty-nine years of marriage. When a spouse dies, the spark does dim. God, my husband, my children, and my grandchildren are the life force within me. My prayers during my parents' deaths and my husband's death were that God protect my heart. After my dad and my mom died, I sensed my heart broken in two places. Eventually, three places were broken within my heart as I pondered whether there is a brokenhearted syndrome or medical term. The term was recognized medically soon after the time I experienced it firsthand.

The "Women of the World in Prayer" inspired by God is asking for prayer for our world and world leaders. Recent events show that all people want freedom and democracy. I have to be mindful not to have a *hardened heart*, and I have to be mindful of my righteous standing before God *if* and *when* I should place myself above other people. This is how I have learned to approach God in prayer, especially when I ask for him to clean house in our country and our world concerning the unseen forces of the *spirits of evil* trying to destroy the name of Jesus and us as Christians. This applies to the *spirits of evil* that cause confusion to humans, leading us to indulge in whatever *sinful nature* at any time or place daily. An example would be greed. It is not fair that the higher-ups get richer and the rest of us pay for their wealth. People do not get it when CEOs pay themselves big bonuses in a span of a year. Reckless bail outs, cover-ups of any safety or health issues, and no one within banks and mortgage companies being held accountable for their role in destroying people's lives and home ownership are another few examples. The government's spending is another major concern unaddressed properly. Who makes the vital spending decisions? Who is accountable? Why don't people receive rewards for conservation and wise spending rather than paying any amount because that's the way it has usually or always been done? What about all government wastes? Self-interest groups greatly concern me, especially now and as before. It is wrong for lobbyists and the recent 2014 money increase from contributors to our government lawmakers to buy votes as the means to get what they want, despite the public outcry to change this corrupt process! It appears that celebrities, companies, higher-up officials, and wealth buy votes in our country. Why? This is why I ask in prayer for you to clean house, Lord. This is wrong!

My prayer has been that God breathe his spirit, his words, and his promises upon our hearts within his world, and turn this economic difficulty around because man does not seem to be able to solve it or bring about the changes we desperately need for us not to have *hardened hearts* and for us to just love God. God knows the intent within our hearts. Do clean house, Lord. Amen.

Chapter Twelve

Music, Praise, and Gratitude

EACH MORNING AS I drove to work, I played certain songs where the words touched my heart. I like different artists and a variety of music. My husband and I had seen Elvis several times, and he was our favorite singer. Whatever songs I picked were the songs where the words resonated within and were precious to my soul. I will mention a few songs and why these songs were sung or played frequently.

I always liked the song "Turn! Turn! Turn!" by The Byrds. The words parallel the Biblical words from Ecclesiastes 3:1-8. This Biblical passage is usually read at funerals.

- "Ave Maria" by Perry Como is sung in Italian and was played over and over each morning as I drove to work as a way to love and connect with Mother Mary.
- "Christ Is Born" is another Perry Como song played during the school year, even though it is a Christmas song. It is a sweet song that glorifies God by the holy names God is known.
- Bette Midler has two songs that are my favorites. "The Rose" tells of enduring love, and
- "From a Distance" is a message for today about God watching us.
- Rod Stewart's "You're In My Heart" is an oldie but goodie. My husband's love remains in my

heart always.

- The Righteous Brothers have been around for a while. Two spiritual songs I love are "He," which speaks of what God made, and "Ebb Tide," which speaks of God as well.
- "Emmanuel" by Amy Grant helped me keep my focus on God and whom he is when I felt like my world was falling apart.
- The day my husband was dying, I played *spiritual* songs by Elvis in the room where he slept. There are too many songs to mention here.
- "O Holy Night" has been my all-time favorite song. I cried and trembled, as I knew I was losing my husband from this earthly world, but I knew my husband was about to enter the kingdom we believe to exist.
- Josh Groban's songs helped me get through my husband's illness and death more than any singer. "You Raise Me Up" was one of those songs! Another song was "To Where You Are," which gave me strength and spoke of *heaven.* I will add "You're Still You" because the words remind me of my husband and the Trinity.
- George Strait sang a song about a father's love. I think of my sons because my husband loved that song. "Love Without End, Amen" is about a father's love being forever. Amen.
- George Strait sings several romantic songs, which my husband knew I favored. They are "I Cross My Heart" and "The Man in Love with You."
- Alan Jackson's song "I'll Try" was my husband and my favorite song by this country singer. My favorite song is "It's All About Him," which is about God, not the singer. Actually, my husband was a huge Alan Jackson fan. Of course, I also like "Little Man," which is about the small-business owners across the United States.

- "I Can Only Imagine" is by Mercy Me. I wish I were in *heaven* to hear and see my husband and the conversations between the Father, Son, and Holy Spirit!

Music is healing. We need to use music more often as an instrument to worship, praise, thank, and show our gratitude to God. I love the hymns sung in church. Today, I feel so sentimental that the songs bring me to tears. "How Great Thou Art" was our dad's, as well as my own, favorite song, and a dear friend from our hometown sang it at his funeral. Mom named several of her favorite songs, but I was not familiar with the ones she named. The same dear friend sang "You'll Never Walk Alone" for us during her funeral at my request. After all, I want my children and grandchildren to believe, trust, and love God to the point that they never doubt that God is as close to them as their next breath during all the storms we call tests and trials. God is that close.

Music is one method of relaxing, and I almost forgot this until I thought about holiday music and shopping during one Christmas season. I thought about getting out of the house many years ago one late Sunday afternoon to go to a local shopping center. Then, something told me to stay home. Later that evening or the next day, I heard on the news that a recent young bride who owned a Mercedes had been robbed and murdered around the time I had thought about going shopping there. The reason I mention this is that my husband had bought a much older model of a Mercedes from his uncle for me to drive. Was that God's protection I sensed? I no longer have the luxury car.

As I slept in bed with my husband, I sensed God so close to him. I saw lights that looked like medium-sized Christmas ornaments in the dark that were clear and bright. They were rested on my husband's chest area. To me, they resembled orbs. Many months after my husband's death, I saw what looked like a cloud of dust floating in a doorway. As I looked closer, I saw so many tiny lights that flickered and what resembled dust floating close to my stomach level. They did not leave for a while, which gave me time to go get my daughter-in-law who happened tobe present that day to witness what I had seen. Orbs visited me too!

Chapter Thirteen

Trials, Tests, Faith, and Strength to Endure

IN 2004, WHEN preparing for our parents' estate sale, my husband called while I was in North Carolina. All that week, mainly at night, I sensed that he would call with bad news later in that week. My oldest brother and next to the youngest brother were present when the phone rang that night. I did not want to answer the call or hear his voice because I dreaded hearing the verdict. My husband's lung cancer had spread to his liver over the years, and he was already in stage four. My husband needed me the summer of 2000 when he found out that he had lung cancer and in 2004 when he found out about his liver cancer. Due to my dad's illness, I needed to be with my parents. The one-day hospice was at our home, and the lady was so helpful in not letting me look back and voice regrets. I only sense the pain and loneliness my husband must have felt upon receiving this type of news and me not being with him both moments. We had talked beforehand at the beginning of that summer about our suspicions concerning the possibility of cancer. He mentioned needing to be close to me on those two occasions numerous times, so I know he needed me more than ever those two trying times in his life.

Around 2011, a couple who had been married a few years longer than my husband and I were having difficulties during one period in their marriage. I sent a card around their anniversary, or maybe Valentine's Day, I do not remember which date, with a note. I had sensed something but did not know what. The friend had told my husband that he had been sleeping on the couch a while, but I did not know any of this. My husband did not mention to me anything the friend had privately told him. One day, I hope to tell our friend that my husband did not betray his confidence. I cared for the couple and hoped a note might help the situation. I told my husband what I had sensed and about the note I had sent when the friend questioned my husband about telling me. We talked about how sensing things may cause conflicts between us down the road. I have talked to the wife since, in 2012, about these details.

An older woman who needed her medicine had gotten away from relatives and was missing for few days. On the way back from one of my husband's final doctor appointments we were on a major highway, and I sensed the woman might be in the thick trees, scrubs, or underbrush near a wooded area. My husband was not feeling well, and I could not use the cell phone due to driving from Norfolk in heavy late-afternoon traffic and trying to comfort him on the trip back home. It was over a week before he began responding well to treatments, and he demanded every moment of my attention day and night. Being human has many flaws, which I ask God to forgive me as I fail to respond. She was found.

My husband has always been friendly and helped other people whenever he could. He was like my father; he liked people. Being a plumber, he helped his friends out over the years, as well as their wives and their girlfriends. In a previous neighborhood of ours, a neighbor's girlfriend sent my husband a card when he was first diagnosed with cancer. However, this woman did not send me a card when my parents died. My husband denied she had sent a card, even though I knew she had. There was no romantic interest, and I will not go into the details except to say that I sensed how the situation between the four of us would end. I decided to speak the truth to this neighbor's girlfriend because of how I felt. Why is it that some women play up to a man and ignore the other woman who may be the wife, girlfriend, or just a companion? My husband asked me how I knew that this woman had sent him a card all those years ago, and I told him I just knew she had.

I did not receive where Saddam Hussein was hiding. However, I did see in a mental vision what appeared to be an off-white or tan, two-story house and what seemed to be a wrap-around front porch. Out of the corner of my right eye, I saw a floating piece of fabric, which seemed white at first. Then, it seemed heavy and dirty like it belonged outside. It seemed to float to a certain spot and stay in the front yard to the right side of the property. I kidded my husband that Hussein was hiding in a well or tunnel covered up by a piece of carpet. That's where they found him under the ground. That is what I sensed with this mental vision.

I have seen how God works to protect situations. For years, I sensed that Osama bin Laden was in Pakistan. I sensed the military base, which seemed odd to me. To be true to the truth and myself, originally I sensed that bin Laden was right under the nose of a military facility and wondered if the government knew or was involved with his hiding whereabouts. I received the distance of around twenty-five miles, but no more than forty, from the military base. From seeing the movie *Zero Dark Thirty*, I may have been sensing the distances that messengers may have traveled to and from his compound. Later in the news, the Navy Seals had been in prior training for years, and the secret mission was in the planning stages.

We now know that some of the Navy Seals train here, which has not been kept secret in the news. Why? I sensed that the pack would be brave and make us all proud. I sensed that they would go together in heartache for the rest of us. It was surprising to me that they survived the raid and went down together in the plane crash, even when "live and die in glory" was what I sensed after the news of the bin Laden capture. God bless our military and their families who are involved, serve, and protect the United States of America. Amen.

As I read the newspaper one morning in January 2012, I saw the silver cord streaming through the shutters toward me with different rainbow colors in a regular rainbow other than the pink, green, and gold mentioned earlier in the rainbow ladder. God continued to show me that he was with me as the first year of my husband's death approached.

It's A Wonderful Life was on during the Christmas season, and I chose not to watch it this year. That was my husband's favorite Christmas program, which he watched yearly. There are few friends, family members, and acquaintances that have been blessed to have been married almost thirty-nine years as my husband and I were. I wish we had had fifteen to twenty more years together like my parents had. When I asked God in prayer why my husband had to die, I sensed the response, "I AM!" God is speaking to me with love that he is in control of all; I have to trust God with this! My husband's death was not to be one of a healing miracle as prayed for in faith. His illness was a test and trial of his faith, trust, and belief in God as a testimony to all of us as his family and as an example in the days ahead. God does not want us to ever be in the darkness about who God is ever. God wants us to be his light in today's world no matter what happens in life, even if there is pain and suffering or loss of a loved one. We are to keep our eyes focused on God! "I AM THAT I AM!" is what the *Spirit of God* spoke within my *spirit heart* often afterwards, and years after, my husband died when I still struggled as his wife with not having my prayers answered concerning my husband's miracle to beat the terminal cancer. I am able to accept that profound proclamation, which I wholeheartedly cherish. I will leave it to God to eventually let me know the reason for why he did not cure my husband of the cancer. One day, God will lovingly answer all these questions for me. What good was to come from his death so young? What was his purpose? I come up with those human questions less frequently now.

A year later after my husband's death, I wanted to have dinner near the Christmas holiday for my sixtieth birthday with friends of ours that had been a couple we had known many years. I had felt concern for our woman friend who had knee damage from a dog accident in mid-to-late July one summer where she was tangled in the dog's leash. Two other lady friends met us at our favorite restaurant. I felt the sadness several weeks before our dinner plans and had asked about her parents and their health. I sensed she was about to lose her dad. Her dad died the day before New Year's Eve. I made a point of talking about him during dinner.

I found my journal and can't believe I forgot this. I was pregnant in 1976 with our youngest child. We were at an Elvis concert in Hampton, Virginia, and I sensed that Elvis would not survive another year due to his weight. He died in 1977. What a blessed voice! What a loss!

In late December 1975, while at the home of my parents in Cary, North Carolina for Christmas, I felt the flutter of new life within me. I felt when *the spirit* of our youngest baby was a fetus within me. I mentioned to my mother and older brother that I knew I was pregnant at that moment. What a blessing to have felt the gift of a child through God! If I felt it with our first child, I was not so aware of that flutter within me. Our youngest son was born nine months later. This verifies that *the spirit of a child* is a person even before the pregnancy has been officially confirmed. I *hope* this word of knowledge answers the question of when a fetus becomes a person. It is the *spirit of the fetus* God has made known as to when a life begins. Amen.

The need for folic acid for women during pregnancy was sensed. Months later, it came out in perfect timing in a health news report. This was over a decade or more ago.

Due to my acid reflux since the '70s, I have drunk lemonade to cut the burning in my stomach, which seems contradictory. But it had been reported in the health news report. This was over a decade or more ago now.

Stem cells were given many years prior in news reports, but I did not know why. Later, it was questioned due to controversial issues. It has now become more common over these years.

There was a motivational speaker who spoke to our school system in 1982. He reminded me of one of the New York Yankee players in looks and build. While listening to him, I sensed that he was a man that travels and motivates so many people. Yet, I felt his loneliness. It seemed to be one of a deep loneliness, even though his speech was one with smiles and jokes. I wished I had gone up to him after his speech to talk to him. He committed suicide in 1982. This was one of my early senses that I had never felt before, so if you know someone is sad make sure you go out of your way to talk to them without a delay. I wonder periodically over the years whether talking to him that day about what I had sensed about his life would have made a difference or not.

I will never know.

I knew who Michael Jordan was and sensed something close to my hometown for some reason. His father was murdered on the side of a road near Hamlet, North Carolina, which is not too far from my hometown. I have driven on that long stretch of road. Michael Jordan had been on my mind, but I do not follow basketball at all. Sorry!

Cancer cells and these numbers were given to me, but I do not know what they mean: 37 / 28, 35.

A friend who had suffered from anxiety was seen in a mental vision, as if in a near-drowning situation last summer of 2011. I saw this friend's face in a whirlpool of foaming water with his face barely surfacing above the water. I sensed an inlet or bay more so than the actual ocean. My husband was in a different hospital in Norfolk at the same time as our friend who was taken to a Virginia Beach hospital after being out swimming. He survived that accident.

Around 1992, I felt a cloud over a former coworker. Later, a relative of the coworker told me the friend was in a car accident on June 21ˢᵗ and had to receive open-heart surgery and pelvic surgery.

I thought the Midwest areas like Iowa, Illinois, Indiana, and Kansas were about to have bad weather, and afterward there was a storm where three hundred people died. This was an early sensation about natural disasters I had never experienced, but nothing more had been given other than the bad weather in 1995.

I had read about a White House scandal, but Ron Brown's plane crash had not been too clear concerning this one because I was not too familiar with this person. However, I do not want to leave out any words of knowledge that I had been given.

Around April 1995, I sensed the Oklahoma area for some reason, but nothing was given about the bomber and the Federal Building. I often wondered what the knowing and purpose was for, as I now think about 9/11.

I thought of a dear, elderly friend's husband in January 2010. Even in his senior years, he was one who liked to party. I sensed that something crazy was about to happen. He committed suicide a month later.

Upon my husband's death on January 9, 2011, God allowed me to see in camera-like pictures by clicks of images how my husband had aged rapidly to become such an old man stricken with cancer. Another hospice lady asked me if he was my father. I showed her how he had looked moments prior to his death and how God had saved all of us from seeing the real effects of cancer upon his body until then. The clicks I saw were as if I was taking pictures with a camera as fast as I was humanly able to focus while one picture was taken and getting ready for the next one to be clicked. My husband's body was full of cancer on the inside, but God did not allow my husband or our family to see the damage upon his body until after his death. What a blessing of God's love and protection!

I seldom dream or remember dreaming, but in April 2012 I had a dream about my husband. I was at the amphitheater on the lawn area. I left and saw one son on his phone while eating at a concession area as I went to the top of a hill. The friend who almost drowned was in his vehicle. There was no passenger in the front seat. I left and went to retrieve my belongings from where I had sat. As I walked to the car, I saw a cafeteria area with lots of tables but with hardly anyone sitting down there. I saw my husband in a gray T-shirt that was given as a gift from my daughter-in-law from her trip to Mexico, and he was wearing jeans and tennis shoes as usual. He approached me with a smile, and we were face to face when the telephone rang at 8:00 in the morning. It was our local newspaper personnel calling. I was upset to have that first and only dream of my husband interrupted!

In 2012, as I was lying on the table in a fairly dark room at our local hospital for another kidney ultrasound, I saw the rainbow ladder, which I had seen periodically before 2004. It came from a ceiling light but was a little different this time. The rainbow ladders were on both sides with what looked like the silver cord in the middle. I was not, nor had been, anxious about this test. This scan was done in reference to the chronic pain I had experienced on my left side for numerous years. The rainbow ladder is a reminder of God's words and God's promises that he cares.

I know who Gary Collins, the actor, is and that he was married to Mary Ann Mobley. I sensed his name in November

2012 several weeks prior to his death. His wife just died recently in 2014.

I never know when or where I will sense any knowledge or information through God. If someone asked me to predict his or her life, I would not be able to do that unless I have a knowing or sense as I have tried to describe as best as humanly possible. First, I take this gift from God as a blessing and any knowledge I have been given very seriously. Second, I pray and talk to God about what knowledge I know and sense in order to verify it is only from him. Third, I am a human being learning how to handle this God-given gift without an owner's manual through this life.

I wanted to write this book about my experiences to help others know and understand that God is in the midst of *all*. I have learned that with whatever knowledge I have received through God, he is in control of *all* circumstances. I just have been blessed to know through God about certain aspects of God's mysterious ways and powers. I have learned that there are times to react and not to react. This writing is about me being a witness for God. God is alive, a living God of today, and not just from the Biblical pages. I am no religious expert on God. I do know that God lives within you and me. *All* I want to do for now is to finish this book for God. Why? This writing is to *glorify* the name of Jesus, God, and the Holy Spirit. God loves you and me so much! God's love is never finished; it is for *all eternity*!

Chapter Fourteen

Faith is a Gift

WEEKS AFTER HURRICANE Sandy hit the East Coast the area was on my mind around December 2012 because of the repeated stories in the news. In my mind's eye and vision, I was seeing a small map of just the edges along the coastal areas labeled New York, New Jersey, and Connecticut. However, right before the Sandy Hook Elementary School shooting, I began to see "CONN" in dark letters to the left of the small map of the previous vision. No other specific or detailed information was given. This did not make any sense to me because all the areas were damaged. However, Staten Island seemed to be in the news more. Seeing the state of Connecticut the way I saw it made me wonder whether something was about to happen in the state. What could it be? I did not know.

Days before the Sandy Hook Elementary School shooting, Sandy, the name of a dear friend, weighed heavily on my mind. The family had just lost their mother, so I kept wondering if I was still just thinking of the family. As you see, the information is like puzzle pieces. I wished I had goggled Connecticut to see about names with Sandy in them. I am not familiar with the state of Connecticut. Like 9/11, I am reluctant to imagine this, but I am to acknowledge that God was in the midst of his dear, little children for good and not causing the *spirit of evil* shooting at Sandy Hook Elementary. God is in control as part of God's divine plan. Don't ask why concerning all of these school shootings and massive slaughtering in the United States and worldwide because I do not know these higher ways of God. I do know that his angels were present; the children and adults were not alone. We are never alone or without God for even a second. At times, we move away from God, but God is faithful to us in spite of our forgetting him. With human eyes, we see the physical body, the shell. *Heaven* had already intervened; their souls were already in the loving arms of our Father. How do I know? The saints were present to take my husband home; the saints were present for all those dear, sweet angels taken from the earth on December 14th. It is my belief those angels were predestined to teach us, break us, mend us, awaken us, and much, much more as a nation. How wonderful to see all the various, religious denominations come together in prayer. That's what I was writing about earlier. All the acts of kindness warm my *spirit heart*. It does demonstrate that God and good triumphs over evil. We are beginning to learn that *all* acts of kindness connect us together as we respond one by one. Our one-to-one responses will eventually become one within God's universe. *If* and *when* we do choose to *collectively and consciously* become one through Jesus, who knows what changes and miracles our world will experience.

All acts of kindness override the unseen *evil spirits*. The words, thoughts, and deeds of our love in our *conscience* are vibrating through the energy of love through God and through God's kingdom. God responds to our heartfelt, love energy. His love is given first to us, then to others, and then through us as God's love vibrates throughout his created, physical world. It is *all* about God's love! This goes along with other learned science lessons.

Why the need for so many guns? Why the need for war? My heart is with the people of the nations that have been fighting for democracy now for many, many years. Let our thoughts and prayers extend to them every day. We do acknowledge that what we do have are God's blessings. One blessing is our freedom. True freedom is only when one believes in Christ, the *cross*, and Jesus's blood that is shed for all. God blesses us.

During the Sandy Hook Elementary shooting weekend, my mind was on Richard Engel, the NBC news correspondent. I usually watch the Channel 10 news most evenings. I had been concerned for some time about all the news people covering Syria and the surrounding areas. Due to safety reasons, it was not reported during that weekend that three news people had been kidnapped. However, I sensed Engel had been captured, but I did not sense the other two journalists. There are times when I acknowledge what I sense and will have to learn to remember in the future when some issues will not be acknowledged ahead of time for security reasons.

I had written some words of knowledge from my journal in another type of book, which I just found and reread. There was a radio announcer who was on an early local morning television show many years ago. I listened to the sound of the television while I was getting ready for work but not too much to each segment, and I had noticed the man's name because it seemed Greek. Again, this was an early happening in my life, and I had to learn how to handle why a name lingered and for what reason. He had a large office in Virginia Beach, and I heard within a few weeks that a gunman had stormed into his office. This family man had been killed. What I sensed was that he would not be on the morning radio program much longer.

Here is another knowing that shows how God is concerned about us in general. I had to take a computer class, which I dreaded. On the way to the first class, I sensed that God was going to send someone I knew to help me with the required class. He did!

I just found another experience in the book. A friend was going to a local sporting event. I had a prior knowing about who was going to win a raffle ticket drawing that evening. It was very tempting to call my friend and and for me to tell her to buy the ticket just before another friend bought their ticket. My husband came home, and I met him at the door telling him who had won and the amount. There is honesty and integrity that comes with knowing such information. I do not get lottery numbers, by the way. The name of the person who was to win the raffle ticket was given. I just happened to know that person.

The Pope just mentioned pets and *heaven* in the news. God loves and is interested in his animals. As I left after visiting a friend, I sensed their pet would not be here much longer. About a week or two later, the friend informed me that the animal had eaten some neighbor's food that was poisonous. I hope to see our family pets Tippy, Cuddles, Tobacco, Stormy, and Jeter in *heaven*, so I *hope* this gives comfort to people who have lost their dear pets. The Pope is right.

I am going to change the situation here. I sensed someone was in a social place and should not have been there due to needing credentials to enter that building. As I sensed someone unknown, or thought of as a possible intruder, I stayed in the front of that building where local security was in place. Luckily, another person in another location in that building had spotted and questioned the individual at that moment and telephoned the incident to the security personnel. The individual tried to pass by among the familiar faces in the crowd while leaving that building. The individual was spotted and followed to the parking lot in a careful manner, the license plate was written down, and the police soon apprehended the person who was down the street. Intruders come into buildings trying to steal pocketbooks or cash more often these days.

Actor Charles Durning was on my mind as I was watching a rerun of *NCIS* during Christmas, and I sensed during the rerun of that episode something concerning the actor and his health. He died that Christmas Eve.

Chapter Fifteen

Who Would Believe?

AROUND MID-JANUARY 2013, Bert Reynolds was on my mind. I happened to watch the television show *Biography* about Sally Fields, and I knew Bert Reynolds had been part of her life. I was surprised to hear on the evening news on the twenty-fifth that he was in the ICU of a Florida hospital at the age of seventy-five.

I had been in prayer to God for many years, asking God to clean house concerning the Catholic Church before I wrote this word of knowledge about the Catholic Church and priests. Many, many years ago, before all the sexual abuse scandals involving young adults, I sensed there was a cover up over numerous decades. In prayer, I would ask God why this had not been exposed because of the children's emotional, physical, and mental abuses. Even today as I watch the news about the cover-up, I still sense the pain that the children feel and have felt *spiritually*. It is my prayer that the guilty priests take responsibility before God. The same goes for any possible leader of the Boy or Girl Scouts, sports' personnel, teachers, and others who work with our innocent angels. This is another prayer request, which is to clean house even in our churches.

As I kept hearing about Mayor Bloomberg of New York dealing with the soda issue, I sensed the loss of a prior mayor to come shortly. I do remember Mayor Ed Koch and sensed his death prior to February 1, 2013.

After my husband died in January 2011, I sensed that in six months or more a good friend of ours would be next in line to become ill with cancer. Due to privacy, I will not elaborate.

There are bits of science information I have already expressed before now. I enjoy learning and watching television programs about the earth and science. What a gift of knowledge about science Albert Einstein was given through God! In my writing, I thought about different scientists and their theories and read more while trying to learn more about their concepts of space, time, and physics in their scientific work. During a time when girls did not think of math and science as girls do today, Carl Sagan, the astronomer and a man of natural science, fascinated me concerning science. Scientists are learning more about our cosmic world. Black holes are of interest to me lately because of the study of galaxies, supernovas, dwarf galaxies, and so forth. I do wish I did understand science better than I do. Mankind may think humans have figured out all about God's creation. We will be surprised to find out how little mankind actually knows. God is our creator. Science must not stand alone with only man as the one who thinks scientists are the true discoverers. It is God who is the creator of his world! He loved us so much as a means of sharing his world with us. Thank you, God.

I feel closer to God when I take the time to meditate in prayer with God. I sense our *conscience* is becoming more mindful to all around us as one. As I meditate by placing my hands on my laps with each hand stretching forward with palms upward and across from the other, I sense the universal energy of God's love we each possess. I know that some people may open their palms upwardly toward *heaven*. During meditation, sensing the loving energy through God is one pathway of the *veil* being lifted in our generation and in generations to come. It is not the meditation as much as it is the aligning of our *spirit heart* to rest and to think of God during any meditation. People fast and just like meditation, fasting leads the people to align themselves to rest and think of God. God's love is given to us through Jesus, just like the disciples and early believers. Why haven't we been taught and why don't we know about such love?

Why haven't we known more about us aligning or positioning ourselves through meditation, which is another name for prayer, concerning God's love? Why haven't we known more about the power of prayer before now and today as it extends into our daily lives? Meditative prayers bring science, God's creation, and love together as one for all of us.

More than ten years ago, as my husband, son, daughter-in-law, another young couple, and I had a meal out together, I thought what a golden boy this young friend of our sons was who had moved from our area. Due to his privacy, I will not describe him or say more. I do not know why good people are stricken with a disease such as paralysis or, like my husband, with terminal carcinoid cancer. Being human, I question why, why not bad people? All I know is that this young friend and my husband may have been chosen by God for some reason because of numerous influences of their lives to all of us who know this young man and knew my husband. As a wife, a mother, and a grandmother I still ask God in prayer why my husband had to die at age fifty-nine. At times I do not understand nor am able to accept why young children and young adults experience diseases and death. Then, I remember all of our loved ones are on loan from God. That makes our loved ones more precious daily. This young adult and his family are in my thoughts and prayers within my heart constantly and daily.

Because I know who God is to me, some may find what I am about to write hard to accept. Praying for people like Saddam Hussein and Osama bin Laden is not of our culture. The *Spirit of God* laid it upon my heart, as a Christian, to learn to pray for these two terrorists, our enemies, and other terrorists of ours because they are children of God as well. As an American, one may think me unpatriotic. I listen to a higher source and obey. Learn to pray for all your own enemies that come before you daily and our enemies of the United States and of the world. One may not like the *sinful nature* one may witness from your or my enemy or enemies. We may consider them to be your or my enemy personally or worldwide, but it is the soul God is concerned with for all of us as his children. This is an example of one of the deeper and higher levels we strive to reach so that we become Christlike as God desires.

It was the end of January in 2013 when Lindsey Vonn, the skier, was on my mind for some reason, and I do not know too much about skiing or that sport. I thought her name was Lynn Vonn, and she had been a concern on my mind. Was she in a Super Bowl or recent television commercial? Her name was brought to my attention with the possibility of dating Tiger Woods. That triggered my sensing her.

My 2013 prayer on February 19th was this prayer from my heart to write today.

I pray, "Father, pour out your breath upon your lands, Holy Spirit. Your people are hurting! Clean house! Do away with spam and scams. Gas prices have tripled and more. Over 70,000-plus humans have died as we all witness war crimes, as if in Hitler's day. In so-called free countries, leaders have their hands in their pockets doing nothing to help their innocent men, women, and children due to greed. Drugs and foods are not properly inspected due to budget cuts. Wise up our United States government to work together daily for the common good for our people and our country in all aspects and for human needs. Hold the guilty accountable for fraud, stealing, misuses of others' dollars, and taking from the poor. You hold the economics in the palm of your hand. Be our God and with your breath grant your grace and mercy and favor to your people once more. My faith lies not in reading the newspaper or hearing the evening news. It is in the pouring out of your love that I ask through your universe and your creation. We are connected by one in you and you alone! I keep reading all this news and hear more daily on the evening news, plus the breaking in or hacking of computers and constant nuclear threats. Keep our eyes and hearts upon you. Thank you, Father. Amen."

Tim Russert was the moderator for *Meet the Press* that I recorded on Sunday mornings. I had sensed sadness to come. What? I came across some misplaced journal notes. I do remember this one after tuning to the program again recently. What a good man who cherished the relationship with his father and family. He died at age fifty-eight in 2008, and I remembered he died a year younger than my husband at age fifty-nine.

At the time of the latest Charlotte Democratic Convention, I was flying out of Charlotte as people were coming to the convention. During the flight, my attention was focused on the metal floor strips, and I wondered why. I was reminded of this when watching the movie *Flight* at home in February 2013. Those metal strips on the floor needed repairs, and it was in the news. Our airplanes need to be carefully inspected.

I had seen the movie *Air Force One* with Harrison Ford when the movie was first released, and also prior to and after 9/11. I had thought that terrorists might use our movies to come up with terrorist schemes. I thought the same while seeing the ad for the movie *Olympus Has Fallen* in March. On March 6, 2013, NBC news mentioned a drone-like vehicle spotted by a commercial airplane in New York air space. Was it just a remote-flying plane or a drone by an amateur in controlled air space? Let us be aware of drones and remotes that look like toys in order to avoid attacks or some type of invasion. Or was I just sensing the affect that the son-in-law of Osama bin Laden was captured and was being brought to the United States secretly to stand trial in the area of his destruction? Now, drones do and will present even bigger issues in 2015.

During the time that the last Pope was retiring, I had my St. Francis of Assisi concrete statue on my mind in March 2013. I was drawn to constantly move it from one spot to another area in my front and back yard like an obsession. Even my grandson touched it, tried to help me move the heavy concrete, and wanted to help me move it for several weeks. I kept wondering why I was so drawn to this statue. I am not of the Catholic faith and had heard the name of the new Pope on the evening news. I had chills when I heard the name Francis and that there had not been a Pope named that since St. Francis of Assisi. I already liked the new Pope for some reason. I heard a sweet, inner spirit say, "You will like the new Pope because you have a lot in common, mostly simplicity." The *Spirit of God* is with this new Pope. There will be changes within the Catholic church, other churches, and for many people as believers in Jesus.

I had a dream less than ten years ago about a couple, which I told my husband about at that time. He may only have mentioned to his guy friend that the dream was about his girlfriend and him, but no details were given because I did not give my husband any details except the location I sensed. The couple was coming out of a building, which I am only able to compare to the front steps of the Admissions Office area at Old Dominion University. However, I sensed that area to be more like the inside of the Higher Education Building off of Princess Anne Road where I have taken classes numerous times. While there, I have sensed the open building to be much like *heaven* with its books of knowledge open to all of us to read for answers. I do not know what the dream meant. I only sense that it was like a life review for the couple because as I was walking toward the steps, I sensed the couple had been through some life-changing event. I do not know what. We did not speak. It was near the end of March 2013, and I have been led to share these chapters with them for some reason.

I had to check the last appearance date of Heidi Klum on CNN with Piers Morgan. I know whom she is due to her modeling career and her marriage to Seal and that they have several children together. I sensed an inner strength other than her being single recently. It was sensed that she would be brave in another way, and that she would come to bat and step up to the plate in a circumstance, but I did not know what or how. During Easter 2013, she was vacationing, although I can't remember the exact location. Due to the rip current, she saved her son, two nannies, and perhaps others who were involved.

Marfan-syndrome was brought to mind in 2013. My middle grandson made an art project of Abraham Lincoln. I kept it because I'm fond of him as a president. It hung on my refrigerator for years. I sensed a deeper connection, which seemed to be not too long after I saw the movie *Lincoln*. It had been several months, and I was not able to shake the connection. All of a sudden, I looked at a friend's child and sensed he might have the same Marfan-syndrome as some experts have alluded that our sixteenth president may have had due to his physical characteristics. I looked at Steve Jobs and thought of him possibly having the same characteristics, maybe Ashton Kutcher as well? I mentioned it to this child's mom, and I am waiting to see if and when the child will be tested.

Around April 2013, I was thinking about Ronald Reagan and Margaret Thatcher. I had on a repeated television special about the Reagan shooting weeks ago. Then, I had thoughts about

Reagan several weeks afterwards. I wondered if Mrs. Reagan might be ill. My next thought was the special connection between the former president and Margaret Thatcher. It had been on my mind to watch the movie with Meryl Streep if and when I could find the movie. Margaret Thatcher died April 7, 2013.

It was near April 6, 2013, that I thought of Rick Warren, who is the pastor of Saddleback Church, and I had read his book, called *Purpose Driven Life*, several years after it had been published. Some time in July or August 2012, I found the book on my brother's bookshelf and read it again while visiting in North Carolina. After losing my husband, I sensed this pastor might be asked to witness about what he preaches. Is this man to be tested concerning his faith? I felt he might be challenged in some manner. How? About what? When? I had a sense of remorse but felt he had done so much with this book and for his church. Was he to be tested with some real trial? I had not known or remembered reading about his son's depression, which led to his suicide.

Renewing our minds was on my mind so strong on April 10, 2013.

- My prayer for our nation is that our *conscience* is renewed daily with God's words and God's promises.
- Pour out your Holy Spirit to renew our *conscience* minds, hearts, physical bodies, spirits, and souls for the *heavenly kingdom* and not of this world nor of our flesh.
- Let us forgive one another, pray for one another, and ask for blessings for those we feel have hurt us and are our enemies!
- Let us put forth effort to renew our *conscience* in order to be more like Jesus daily.

I watch or tape *Jeopardy* as one of the ways to stimulate my mind like I do as I try to work crossword puzzles daily too. I had a feeling that Mr. Trebek was going to be hurt in some fashion, but I did not know what. It was in the news that his hotel room had been robbed and some damage had been done to one foot in 2012. I hope that Mr. Trebek does not retire too soon from the show because he has been with this educational program for many years. The fans appreciate such an excellent job he has done. Thank you!

In 2013, I had not heard of the Jackie Robinson movie *42* being made. I am a Yankee fan, but Jackie Robinson had been in my thoughts for many years. I wondered why this man's life and his wife's life and courage had not been made into a movie after all these years. I am learning more about the man and his wife because I was not born in 1947 but in the early '50s. However, I did live through the 1960s in the south. The *spirit* of this man and this woman lives today through that movie. I was so moved that toward the end of the movie I was shaking with such overwhelming emotions because of the display of Jackie and Rachel Robinson's faith and courage. What prejudice and hatred they endured! Jackie Robinson and Branch Rickey, the owner of the team, were inspired by their faith to show that *God built* Jackie as a prelude during the Civil Rights Movement. Many African Americans endured discrimination, racial slurs, and hatred. Jackie Robinson believed in *patience* for change to come. We still have a long way to go. I am looking forward to seeing Jackie Robinson's life in more detail in a documentary or a movie by Ken Burns in the future, so that my grandchildren, other younger children, and generations to come will know our American history through the lives of the people who lived it. Mr. and Mrs. Robinson were examples of good triumphing over evil.

During the weekend of April 13, 2013, I was not feeling well due to my chronic medical issue, but I wondered why I felt heaviness come over me, like once before, and that something was about to happen. I could not shake that dark sense. My older brother's birthday was that Monday, the fifteenth. I could not make myself go to the store to buy a card, but I knew I would talk to him that day. By late Sunday evening, and only for a split second, I thought of 9/11. Little by little, I was sensing a possible location: the Boston area. If I had known or been aware of the Boston Marathon, it would have made more sense to me. One question that came to me after the bombing that day was whether water and boats surround all of Watertown. My first thought was wondering whether all docks, boats, and waterways were checked during the neighborhood searches.

God is bringing us together. We are all connected and shall be connected through God, even though the spirits of evil bring terror to our world.

I have no concrete evidence, but I sense there are more terrorist cells that have been in the United States for numerous years. They may be in our many professional capacities such as medical fields or in universities as professors or students, as it has been uncovered, or people living in our rural, small towns or from any walk of life that we are not aware of or do not question.

As a nation, we need to pray, "We believe in Jesus; we trust in Jesus. We trust him. We trust Jesus. Amen."

Chapter Sixteen

There Are No Coincidences

IN APRIL 2013, I *missed the mark* as I was working in the yard on a cool day, which we had not had in the area for a while. I sensed that I should go visit a friend that Saturday or Sunday. I continued to do yard work. The friend had fallen that weekend and could not get off the floor until a neighbor knocked down the door. The friend is fine. Yes, I *miss the mark* when I do not obey what I sense. I apologized to my friend because I had failed to respond to that inner voice.

When I mentioned 9/11 in chapter 7, I forgot to mention that I had sensed over the years that some of the 9/11 wreckage, body remains, or something else might be lost and not discovered. If so, I *hoped* my prayer would be answered for any recovery. What a surprise to hear about the large plane debris found in an alley in New York after all these years.

In June 2013, *The Sopranos* actor, James Gandolfini was on my mind, even though I only periodically watched the television show over the years. Several weeks before his death, *The Sopranos* was on my mind. I hope this gives his teenage son and family comfort to know that I sensed his death to come. He seemed like a nice guy. What a loss for his family when someone with such talent leaves us at an early age in life. He seemed like a gentle and shy giant of a man.

A month earlier, in May 2013, as I continued my prayer meditation with God, I saw stained church windows in front of me that were part of my visualization over the years. Now I have seen a white *cross* within the stained windows, which had not been part of my meditation at the beginning, as part of my daily and *consciously* renewed mind, spirit, heart, soul, and body connection through God. The *cross* is always in my thoughts. Now, it is a vision during my time with and through God.

During the spring of 2013, I had not seen or talked to my husband's best friend on a regular basis as I had done before my husband's death. I thought of how he might be doing since then. In my mind, I thought it might be nice to run into him somehow. As I left a dental appointment, I saw his vehicle go past as I was leaving. As I left the parking lot, he was caught at the stoplight. I pulled up beside him and rolled down my window to speak for a few seconds before the light changed. It was nice to see and talk to him. It was not a coincidence. It was an answer to a silent prayer by one friend to check on another friend.

That June 2013, I was to have another similar coincidence a few weeks later. After looking at our picture albums, I had thought of a couple that my husband and I had known from our Virginia Beach Little League days. I had seen the couple many years ago as I walked out of a store, and they entered. It was weeks after my husband and I had just found out about his liver cancer in 2004. At that moment, I did not stop to tell them. The woman friend happened to call as a political volunteer one afternoon. It was not a coincidence and was nice to talk her since the league had been part of our lives from T-ball to Super Seniors.

Because of thinking about our children in schools, it is my prayer that the Holy Spirit touches our conscious and subconscious minds concerning what is important in today's society. Society is of the secular world where fame, beauty, wealth, and worldly possessions are of value. Look at the way women dress so provocatively these days with fewer clothes on than the next female, as if to be the one to grab the headlines ahead of others in the news, videos, television programs, and more. It is a shame that such pressure is placed upon woman today to have to compete in that way. Singers, actors and actresses, television programs, and more flood the shows we watch with such nudity and with the homosexual lifestyle, cheating and affairs, and so forth. Athletes, models, movies, the latest electronic equipment, the rich and famous, and much more are like idols rather than people seeking to know God by reading the Bible and wanting a personal relationship with God. It will be the Holy Spirit that will open our whole hearts, whole minds, whole spirits, whole souls, and whole bodies to know Jesus is not of this secular world. It is only through who God, who brings satisfaction through our lives, not this secular world we love as humans.

During either June or July 2013, after a friend was diagnosed with cancer, I sensed that a friend's wife was next. After my husband's death, I sensed that I might be next in line with a health issue. I was not to follow right away, but the friend's wife was. I mention this because after this friend's wife, I sensed Randy Travis. As I mentioned in the chapter about music and songs, my husband played his music often. You can read about our favorite song about growing old together in chapter 12. Randy Travis lived less than thirty miles from my hometown. My uncle used to kid me each time I saw him by teasing that Randy Travis was a famous neighbor. All of this was sensed before hearing about his recent heart infection and hospitalization. My thoughts and prayers go out to a fellow Carolinian.

I do like the *Law and Order* television program. Again, I had been watching reruns during the summer of July 2013. Dennis Farina played the role of Detective Fontana. I sensed his death, which was July 22, 2013.

Robin Williams was on my mind, and I wondered why. I knew his new television series had been cancelled and wondered how he was dealing with that. I wish I had been more in tune about his depression and illness that led to his death.

Chapter Seventeen

Confirmation of Word of Knowledge and Discernment

THERE HAVE BEEN many times when God will speak to me throughout the day and as I awake the next morning. I do hear confirmation about God's prior words of knowledge given to me. Again, I do hear preacher's sermons lately that are preaching about what my *master lessons* have been, and I want to acknowledge Reverend Creflo Dollar of the World Changers Ministry in Atlanta, Georgia as one of the preachers who speaks similarly to the words of knowledge as I finish this writing. Whether I used the word *knowing, sensing, an inner spiritual voice, energy,* or other terms, I was receiving the words of knowledge, the same *master lessons* being taught to me. Within a day or week of my words of knowledge, I have heard other preachers recently preach what I had just been taught as well. Over the years, it was, and still is, important that I learned to question and to discern whether what I received or had received was through God. Thank you for boldly preaching and being an instrument of God whom I connected to and I corresponded to from Virginia to Georgia. However, I am not a Biblical scholar or preacher. *The Answer* is written to *glorify* the name of Jesus. Thank you, Rev. Creflo Dollar, for preaching about the New Covenant today. That is the message through God given to us to spread. In agreement, one day everyone will hear and accept

Jesus. Every knee will bow before Jesus in *heaven* before God. Amen.

I will end by saying that I do repeat certain words and phrases often because they need to be said to the point that they are remembered. It is the same with one's gut feeling, extrasensory perception, and one's gift of words of knowledge. When someone, or a thought that one perceives, is gifted through God, do go to God in prayer to make sure it is of God. I will conclude by saying that I am a human being like everyone else and do rebuke what is not of God with strong and loud words. This book is offered to believers and nonbelievers, so God is remembered and not forsaken by anyone who wants to rededicate their lives to God or accept God for the first time as their Lord. There is no manual that comes with living life. I dedicate this book to the One who is precious to me as I live my life: The Father, the Son, and the Holy Spirit. Shalom. Amen.

Chapter Eighteen

My Prayerful Meditation

PRAYERFUL MEDITATION IS not a gimmick of the New Age or a Western civilization tactic. I practiced prayerful meditation, even before I knew exactly how to do it correctly. I chose a comfortable place to sit and was silent because I needed to have time alone at the end of most days. I thought about a Bible passage I had just read and sometimes recreated that Biblical passage in my mind. I imagined how I might react or what I might say if I saw Jesus, heard his sermons, witnessed his miracles, met Jesus face to face, or had the chance to talk to our Messiah. Meditation was the beginning of another lesson I learned through my Master Teacher. As I closed my eyes, I learned that it was not only a nap or a five-minute break, but also, a lesson on how to learn to take as much time as necessary to rest in Jesus.

"God, I am silent and still before you. You are within me; I am within you. We are one," I whispered.

As time went by, I became more creative by imagining being surrounded by a lit white candle that represented God's protection. I would light a candle when I first meditated and still light candles from time to time as a reminder of God's protection and light around me daily. I sat up straight in a chair with my feet flat on the floor, had my right hand laid flat on top of my right thigh, and my left hand laid flat on top of my left thigh. Next, the importance of each deep breath eventually became clearer to me. As I took one deep breath, I inhaled as much air as I could. I held it as long as I could and exhaled the air slowly. I did the same for the second and third deep breath. At first, I would take an extra, very deep breath or more if not as relaxed as I needed to be in that moment. Afterwards, I imagined I was resting at my favorite relaxing spot, even though I was still at home. Over time, I imagined different and various locations that were just as effective and more calming than finding quiet time in my home. I wanted to get comfortable talking to God, which led to God's holy place.

Initially, my favorite place to be calm was the beach where I love the sound of the ocean. That progressed and I chose to relax while imagining lying in a hammock facing the ocean and feeling a gentle breeze. From there, I felt cozy by dreaming of long, flowing, white linen curtains that were sheer. In the background, I hear soft music that soothes me. The floor is of beach sand, and the walls and ceiling are open, as if I am sheltered on all four sides and above from any hot weather or storm. I know God's presence. I sense God in nature as I enjoy swimming freely with dolphins in the warm ocean water.

Pick what you love and where you are comfortable being during your talks with God. I know and love God through his world that he shares with me. What is beautiful to you? I love seeing even a single blade of grass and a single petal on a garden plant. As I think of nature, God's love fills me from the top of my head to the bottom of my feet. You will want to fill your renewed *conscience* daily with thoughts of God and prayers to God.

Move downward to your heart once you acknowledge and believe God as being part of your *conscience* and renewed thinking within your mind. To me, it has always been about our hearts. Why? To me, the heart is where God transforms us through his love. The heart of God is that energy we call love. Love is so powerful. We use the word so casually. It is God's love that transforms mankind. As God's love flows through your mind, completely fill your mind and heart with renewed thoughts of God's love, with prayers of gratitude, and with thankfulness for your loved ones, friends, and for yourself. My realization is by the faith of Jesus, the name of Jesus, who Jesus is to me, and by knowing that the power of God is always within me. Grace is offered beyond measure. I did not deserve God's grace nor did anything to earn it; I already had grace. How? Grace is God's free gift bestowed upon us. All we have to do is believe and accept God's daily gift. God's *grace* is sufficient for each new day. Jesus is *grace*. What a beautiful Biblical principle taught through meditation!

Prayers may be simple and said with honest words. Prayers should come from the heart. I believe God honors heartfelt prayers. This is when and where the lesson of people needing our minds, hearts, spirits, souls, and physical bodies to be renewed daily with God's words and God's promises was taught to me through God. Remember how important your heart and my heart are to God. I do believe God searches and looks within our hearts, as only God is able to do. As with the mind and heart, God will reveal his truth, his love, and his light to the whole person. God wants you to be as his child.

Move on down to your stomach area, and fill your physical body and *conscience* with renewed thoughts of the truth of God, his love, and his light. Keep moving down to your other body parts as long as you prayerfully meditate about giving your *all* to God. The process will take time to saturate your whole body. I do say that my healing was given over 2,000 years ago and so is prosperity, my salvation, and all my needs. It is done through Jesus! Sometimes, I would start at the top of my head and speak to God about my migraine headaches and other parts of my body that I believed to be healed, asking to see that healing and waiting patiently by resting in the finished works through Jesus. I no longer have migraines. Some days, I will start at the top of my head for what healing I ask for, believe to see, and wait patiently as I pray for healing all the way down to the tips of my toes. Other times, I would start at my toes and do the reverse as I ended up speaking to God about his healing by closing my prayer at the top of my head area.

I am guilty of this. One important lesson is not to moan, groan, or fret over my health or any ailment. Now, I do say that *all* is well; I am whole. This belief through prayerful meditation may take time to comprehend, but do practice as you learn this process and proceed by turning your *all* to God. Restored health may or may not be immediate through God. I do not know why some people are healed and others are not. I have had a chronic health problem for years and do not know why God has not healed me after over forty years. Isn't this a way for us to learn how to give ourselves, by submitting ourselves to God?

An important note of wisdom is that it is always necessary to speak out loud before any prayerful meditation and that you will not accept any knowledge unless it is through God. Be self-assured and forceful when you speak those words because your words have power through Jesus. You do not want to accept or claim any *spirits of evil.* I have learned to command and demand only Jesus who is holy to be present during my prayerful meditations. You, too, have the power through Jesus to accept and claim that which is holy and of God.

I am now at the point where I see beautiful, stained glass windows, as if in a church. I know the reverence and sacredness of Holy God. Prayerful meditation is immediate to me now wherever I am. I have now seen the *cross* within the windows I described. The relationship with God grows deeper each day. While reading this book, you will later understand when I say that I am not the same on any given day. I am evolving while talking and walking with my best friend daily. God is within you, and God is within me every second of each day. We are one with God, and we are all connected.

I pray, "Lord, here I am. Speak to me. This is our time alone. It's just you and me. Thank you for your holy words and promises. Teach me through your Holy Spirit. Shalom. Amen."

You may want to go ahead and read the chapter titled "Mind, Spirit Heart, Soul, and Body" before and after learning to prayerfully meditate. Rest in the Lord.

Chapter Nineteen

Mind, Spirit, Heart, Soul, and Body

YOU MAY WANT to read this section before and after learning about prayerful meditation. When it comes to thinking about Jesus, you are not able to separate the mind, heart, spirit, soul, and physical body. First, I was taught about the mind. Knowing this is our mental intellect, I had to become even more aware of how important my own personal human feelings, wants, thoughts, and actions are affected if I am not daily reading the words and promises of God. Be on guard each moment of every day about what garbage is taken in that crosses your mind and learn to self-talk, which may seem strange at first. Self-talk is just saying words verbally out loud to teach your mind not to believe what bad thoughts filter or seep into your mind. The *spirits of evil* will try to rob you of your joys by tricking you to think the opposite by depression and comments of failure rather than success, not being capable of a job rather than being creative, not being loved rather than to believe that God loves you, staying in financial distress rather than asking God to be your source through his abundant supply, and the list continues every second of every day. Whatever you hear in your mind that is negative, learn to say aloud the opposite words, which are positive. With constant practice that becomes part of you, do say out loud that you are not accepting any particular garbage you are listening to at that moment.

There is more about self-talk at the end of this chapter. Do self-talk every time, even if you have not ever heard of this concept or if you and others don't use it right now. I will explain self-talk as a learning technique I used as a teacher that worked. As a Christian or nonbeliever, do say out loud that this is not of God and that you accept only what is of God. Be assertive when you voice your power over the *spirits of evil* or any sinful thoughts. The chapter titled "Evil in God's World" will go more in detail about the *spirits of evil* and about our other human challenges. These negative thoughts that come into your mind want to govern and control you. The most important lesson taught by the *Spirit of God* is that we need to renew our minds daily and by reading the word of God and the promises of God in the Bible. Why? The *spirits of evil* try to attack our minds. They will succeed if you do not know God. The *spirits of evil* try to destroy the children of God. Go to the Bible for God's divine help, God's power, God's refreshing of your mind, and God's contentment and peace for you.

Also, you will be successful and prosperous in your life by being led by God and not the garbage that is in your mind. I believe that our own destruction and that of others first comes from the wicked thoughts within our minds from the *spirits of evil*. If people did not think of or listen to such evil or act upon these *spirits of evil*, evil would be deflated, wiped out, disposed of, and permanently vanished. It is only by the renewing of our minds daily and throughout the day that we will become more Christlike. It is my *hope* that self-talk is being used each time there is doubt in our minds. Say aloud, "I believe in you, Jesus," and surrender it *all* to God.

Here is what I was taught about the *physical body*. Knowing this is how we live in our physical world, our body is encased within our human flesh. We identify with the human flesh because we are in this secular world. In today's world, our own physical appearance seems to be the refection of who we think we are to ourselves and to others. That is why our human flesh is in constant conflict with our soul. It is just the way it is as human beings. There is so much more to learn about health issues, medicine, research, and so forth as all relate to the body. Just know that your body is *sacred* to God. God created you and me out of his own image. That's why we are holy to God.

Next, I was taught about the *soul*. I am still being taught about the soul. Our soul tries to copy what is part of the human flesh. God was part of my everyday thinking within my *conscience*. What about the soul? Now, I know that it is important to be aware that it is our *conscience* that corresponds through God, which is of his ethical and morals standards. As a young child, knowing between right and wrong was taught. Was God just the *conscience* part of our *spiritual* being? I believed as a teenager in the whole connection of the human being, which is the mind, heart, spirit, soul, and physical body. I knew all were in connection with the others only because we are the total package to God. Each day was special in the sense that I wanted my mind to be renewed; I didn't want to make the same mistakes again and not please God. I wanted my heart to be pure before God as I sensed his heart was pure love for me. I was scratching the surface of what the word Christian meant. I knew there was more and that I would learn more about his truth and light. Thinking about God was tucked within my daily thoughts and prayers. I sensed that God already knew I searched my soul to know him.

I bared my mind, heart, spirit, soul, and physical body through Jesus. I knew that my life as a young child was maturing when I got closer to graduating high school. My life was always in God's hands. Everything was in his hands! Did I trust him to lead me? Would I be going down my own path or his?

"God, show me you are real in today's world," I asked often as I sought God.

"I would never ask this to test or doubt you. I want what you offered your disciples!" I said as I sought him through child-like faith.

"I believe there is more about you, Jesus, God, and the Holy Ghost than what today's preachers are preaching," I simply stated.

Lastly, in prayerful meditation I learned the *heart* and *spirit* are separate, yet in correspondence with one another. Our hearts do connect through God. Our spirits connect through God. Over time, I learned and believed to say that my *spirit heart* connects through God. Other times, I do say my heart and my spirit connect through the *Spirit of God*. I know and believe the heart and spirit are indeed separate. However, as my heart and spirit did respond through one another, that is my connection as one through Jesus. I believe that is the way to the true path to God. God is love. It is God's love that connects us. It is the *heart* and *spirit* of God through us that connects God through to us. It is the heart and spirit of God that connects God through me. This is his truth. I am still being taught by the *Spirit of God* daily and will evolve as I still grow and mature as a believer through Jesus. My love for God only grows deeper each day. We need to revere the word "love"; love is *sacred* to God.

At times, I still use self-talk when I think of being under the Old Law and under the Old Covenant in the Old Testament. I say aloud, and inwardly know that I am under the New Covenant where *all* my sins are paid in full *by the faith of Jesus* and the *cross*. All that I am is because of Jesus. My self-talk is my way of staying connected to God in a positive way rather than letting any negativity of an offense by a person or situation cause me to have or keep a *hardened heart* toward that person or situation. I do say to God that I turn all over to him time and time again *if* and *when* a hurt feeling emerges. I know that if I do speak, or have spoken, the truth that is all I need to do to correspond through to God. Shalom. Amen.

I will summarize about self-talk, so you understand why I know it is important. Self-talk was used by me as a teacher. For example, I used self-talk as I taught each step in math from the process of simple division to long division. The importance to students was shown as they said the directions out loud through each step of the division process. This allowed the student and me to hear what the student was thinking while solving the problem. I could automatically redirect their way of thinking by suggesting a higher or lower number to use or ask if addition or subtraction was the next step, and all these means by learning self-talk were ingrained into their way of thinking as another division problem was presented that was to be re-taught or if the student was ready to work a longer division problem on their own. Self-talk is vital every second of every day as we determine what garbage we choose to believe, to listen to, and to filter into our minds.

Chapter Twenty

Evil Within God's World

WHEN READING THE Bible, I became more aware of phrases such as "in the midst," "out of the midst," "through the midst," "within the midst," and so forth. Those phrases caught my attention more than ever before while reading my Bible. This was evidence and proof to me that God has always been present with all generations throughout his creation. There were appointed kings set on thrones by his hand and dethroned by that same hand for his reason in history. History has been on his timetable, and people have been scheduled to do God's will in the midst of circumstances and situations whether we acknowledge or not that God sees all evil and knows of all evil yesterday, today, and tomorrow. Jesus never promised us a rose garden; Jesus warned us that we would face tests, trials, and tribulations. What would we learn *if* and *when* we are never given the opportunity to grow? I wonder why it is through each difficult time in life that we go to God needing to speak to God as we have never done before experiencing suffering?

I say in prayer, "Jesus, I am hurting so bad right now because of ______________. I ask you to wrap your arms around me with your love. There is no way I have the strength to bear this ______________. Lift me up and do give me *grace* to face ______________ through your love. Grant me *mercy* to endure __________. And I do thank you for your *favor* as I rest by faith in you as my Savior, Jesus. Shalom. Amen."

It is my personal prayer that people everywhere know God and that God blesses all. We are to be his disciples, as the followers of Jesus Christ, of today. Because of prosperity, which is through *grace* freely given through God, it is my personal prayer that God's believers know to ask, ask in faith, and believe God is our one and only supplier. God is our supplier where his *all* is available in increase and abundance. Your answers to prayers may or may not necessarily automatically arrive upon that one request but still within God's will. It will be done *if* and *when* God desires his will and plan fulfilled for you and me. His supply may even come from a person God has positioned to help you with a certain need that you do not expect. God uses supernatural and unexpected people, events, situations, circumstances, and whatever and whenever he chooses and wills. God manifests to his children. His will and due time is different than our thinking and ways. The hand of God will not limit whom and what. God is love; God provides.

These two words continued to catch my attention as I read my Bible. To have a "hardened heart" is to be a person who does not trust God. Not trusting God blocks out and cancels out the ability to know that our source is God. It is because of our selfish, impatient, prideful, self-effort, and human nature. God understands that about us. God does love us forever.

Hardened hearts are other words to describe hate, or to abhor, which is a Biblical term. We are to abhor evil. However, Jesus taught us to pray for our enemies. I am going to ask you to consider the daily warfare Christians *spiritually* fight. Imagine, as the children of Christ, we are his Christian soldiers. It is exciting to grab hold of the idea that I will stand for Christ. Just as we are called to pray and stand for Israel, we are called to stand and fight for Christ. Keep reading because you will become aware and acknowledge the inner conflicts we face still today. The devil's spiritual warfare was defeated over 2,000 years ago. Yes, the evil force called the devil is already defeated. Jesus won! Jesus won the battle, and the devil has been defeated for eternity. How? Jesus. It is by his *grace*, so there is nothing we need to do by our self-effort. Read and reread the chapter about our minds, hearts, spirit, soul, and physical body because the *spirits of evil* are of the devil, and other *evil spirits* by certain names bring devilish thoughts as garbage into our minds and try to keep us within our thoughts. The *spirits of evil* are the negative tapes or recordings that keep playing over and over in our minds. Think out loud and use self-talk that you do not want that garbage to collect or clutter in your mind. When we are not reading the words of God and not reading about the promises of God, *evil spirits* do attack. Why? We become vulnerable as a human. Do we have any real defense against evil but Jesus?

Yes, think of what Christians already possess through Jesus. *Grace* was not earned; *it* is God's free gift of his love to each of us. Grab hold of that free gift, and do not let it go! God loved and does love us so much to send his beloved Son to die in our place. *Grace* abounds because Jesus is our strength. Without Jesus, we have no strength. As a Christian, I want to align myself to be in a close union with Jesus, and it is that position through Christ that I am able to stand and stand boldly against the unseen forces and powers that are *evil spirits* in this world.

There are many names for the devil who was cast out of *heaven* with his demonic angels. Evil, or what we call Satan, the devil, Powers of the Air, Serpent, Deceiver of the whole world, and other names are described as read in Revelations12:1-2 as the corruptive one of *all spirits of evil*. This *evil spirit* is called the Creature of Light because the *evil spirit* is able to attract, deceive, and captivate the children of God *if* and *when* we are not in prayer or reading God's words or claiming or accepting God's promises of his love and truth. Picture the *evil spirit* going before God in *heaven*, trying to be against us as God's children. God is on our side and protecting us. I visualize that the *evil spirit* did not win in *heaven*, so the *evil spirit* tries to invade our minds, our hearts, our spirits, our souls, and our physical bodies with his greatest evils for all mankind. That is why we need to know the power and authority in the name of Jesus. I will repeat this *master lesson*. That *evil spirit* will invade us anytime and anywhere when we are weak, sick, depressed, lonely, hopeless, and vulnerable human beings. Be vigilant in prayer to guard against anyone and anything that tries to bring division within a family's home, a neighborhood, a community, a city, a state, a nation, and the world.

Christians want to believe only in the devil as a religious figure that churches presented. What about the *spiritual warfare* in high places? There are *evil spirits* of darkness. These principalities and spirits do try to weaken us as humans. These are ones of confusion, deceit, trickery, condemnation, guilt, and any and all precise plans to defeat Christians when we think we have *fallen from grace*. Have you heard the words "amazing grace"? God offers his free gift of his amazing *grace* when we do *miss the mark* because he offers *grace to grace*. That is who the Trinity is within us to the end of our life. Because I acknowledge God's *grace*, I do not want to trust myself; I trust Jesus. We *fall from grace* each time we do not stand boldly believing and boldly having faith that Jesus has already paid the price. It is done! We think we are the ones in control of our life. We go back to the Old Covenant, the Old Law. This is the *spiritual warfare* we face. The *spirits of evil* know and believe in Jesus. They still attack! In 2015, and in the years to come, God's children will be under attack as never before in history. Before I ended this writing, I asked in prayer if there was anything to be clarified or added. Because I am human and when younger, my first thought was to blame God when I saw or heard about any bad thing happening in our world. The bad happenings are those of the unseen *spirits of evil* that God is blamed for daily. God is love and wants the best for us.

It is my prayer that we believe in God's words and God's promises. *Grace* overflows when knowing that *heavenly* knowledge. I saw "GRACE-MERCY-FAVOR" in black, bold letters. I am still evolving to know how important each words is and what each means. I do know that these words teach me more about God's blessings. I do not have to do anything but believe *by the faith of Jesus*, and that is to believe in the name of Jesus and who Jesus is to me. None of us deserve his *grace*, but it is freely given. None of us deserve his *mercy*, but it is extended to us each new day. None of us deserve his *favor*, but God loves us. All of us have taken Jesus for granted, and I confess that I have done that as well. It is a scheme of the evil forces in our world today. I *hope* this helps us to understand what we are up against as humans each second of every day. Learn to stop the tapes or recordings in your mind and say out loud that evil garbage is not only put on pause, it is forever deleted. Jesus reigns through me! My mind does focus upon Jesus daily!

That is why I believe so much in our *collective conscience* through to God. Christians and nonbelievers will gain the knowledge that negative thoughts, condemnation, and other destructive means are of these *spirits of evil* through deception and trickery and every way possible to try to get us to think differently within our renewed minds, hearts, spirits, souls, and physical bodies concerning the strength and might of Jesus. Why? These *evil spirits* do not want us to believe Jesus is victorious now and forever. *Evil spirits* do not want Christians to believe in the strength and might of Jesus. As Christian soldiers, we are to stand and to stand boldly for Jesus. If any or all *evil spirits* try to get a Christian or nonbeliever not to believe in Jesus and his finished work over 2,000 years ago, that *evil spirit* has used deceit, trickery, and other means to cause us to *fall from grace* and away from Jesus. We are forgiven of all our sins yesterday, today, and tomorrow. How do I know? It is knowledge through God's words and God's promises. I rest in the finished works of Jesus. It is *by the faith of Jesus* I have learned to love, trust, and believe, which is not my faith alone. It is *by the faith by Jesus* only. God is already working on my behalf whether I need his supply for comfort, contentment, peace, food, clothing, money, housing, physical healing, or whatever else I need in my life. Learn to rest in our Lord.

Jesus is the answer. Jesus is my answer. Jesus is your answer. It is by the faith of Jesus, through believing in God's word, and through believing in God's promises. It is by humbling ourselves and going before God that I have learned to still watch out for the numerous and various kinds of *evil spirits* that invade our minds to cause road blocks or stumbling blocks each second of every day through life.

In prayer I now say, "Father, thank you for your strength and might that I am able to stand boldly knowing I am your Christian soldier in the battle of the unseen *evil spirits* that try to defeat me because they still want to deceive, trick, and destroy your children. You already won! You are victorious! It is your victory at the *cross*. It is finished. It is done through your blood.

Thank you for your *grace, mercy, and favor* each day. Pour

out this knowledge to your Christian soldiers in today's world. By the faith of Jesus and God's words and promises, we know we are already aligned, in position ready to fight, and victorious over our own mental battles individually and *collectively and consciously* through the name of Jesus. Shalom. Amen."

Yes, if we *collectively and consciously* pray as a nation and as a world against all our *spirits of evil* who do continuously try to possess and defeat mankind, people of all nations will see changes we will make as one through Jesus. I repeat *hardened hearts* so many times in this reading because it is mentioned in the Bible as well. This is an indication that Jesus is not remembered or spoken about in our renewed minds. We all are guilty of possessing *hardened hearts* because we do not always act Christlike in our daily lives as human beings. For me, this was a new and hard concept to learn after all these years. We need to understand how valuable and important this *master lesson* is to us, so we do not grieve the heart of God.

This is why we need prayers back in our public lives, in schools, in city hall meetings, and everywhere. We are up against *evil spirits* as part of the human race if we do not turn back to acknowledging, remembering, and speaking the name of Jesus. It is through knowing the Son of God and what Jesus truly means to us. God loves us. God wants the best for all his people. God abides with us in the midst of fear, torment, diseases, poverty, crimes, weather disasters, hatred, human abuses, and other disturbances, which are the *spirits of evils* as stumbling blocks to destroy us. We have the power and authority to recognize each evil that is attacking and speak out loud and with a firm voice to command and demand each *evil spirit* to be demolished, pulverized, crushed, gone forever, rebuked, banned, and more in the name of Jesus *if* and *when* we stand bold to do so. I hate evil as God hates evil. All evil does is grieve the heart of God.

Collectively and consciously it is up to all of us to be God's agents of change in our homes, neighborhoods, communities, states, countries, and world. We are to be united as one through Jesus to stomp out whatever evil we see or hear. What if we had leaders that united the United States and our world to pray with us daily as a nation against fires, floods, natural and manmade disasters, economic difficulties, domestic violence, and local, state, and national issues too big to be solved by men and against our stalled political changes and self-serving government that supports a few people and against everything too big to solve by mankind alone? What if all denominations will come together as one to pray as one against terrorism? This is what is politically correct in God's eyes! We need to cut out the red tape and monitor censorship and question court cases against speaking the name of Jesus at all local, state, and national levels when it comes to praying in the name of Jesus as a people for our world that we inhabit together. Admit it, we are in bad shape as a nation! I do believe in the separation between church and state. However, our forefathers believed in God. How did it work for them but we can't see that it would work for us today?

I pray this for all of our children and for all of our grandchildren. We are living in the world God created for us. We are to stand up against whatever evil and whatever enemy to boldly announce there is no more room or place here for demonic *evil spirits* or for any more pain directed at or towards God's children. Together, and only through Jesus, will we be victorious and eliminate suffering, hurt, and pain for all mankind.

Because of the recent racial unrest in our country, this does not mean anyone has the right to destroy anyone's business or anyone's property or set fires during demonstrations or any other damage or vandalizing. Do you believe that you have that right to do this as an individual? If not, then do not do this when you are in a group. You know it is wrong to do this. No, it is not okay to do this even when everyone else is doing it in a crowd or riot. Stealing is stealing, no matter what. It amazes me when a person has been taught what is morally right and wrong but thinks God is not watching. The Bible mentions that his eyes are moving back and forth across his creation, and he sees and knows what you and I do. Shalom. Amen.

The *spirits of evil* tried to attack me with negativity while writing this book. Why write this book? You are just a wife, mother, and grandmother. No one will want to read your book. It has all been said before; it will just be another religious book. God granted me the passion to obey when I heard this negativity and much more within my mind, but I chose to defeat God's enemy.

We are witnessing the *collective consciousness* I write about as we see the worldwide Paris demonstration against our enemies called terrorists. Let us join hands and pray together for our enemies and against hatred. We are not to fear. God is not of fear. It is with our united love and in prayer that we stand firm as one against worldwide hatred. In 2015, expect to see and experience God's goodness that we may have either taken for granted and ignored. In 2015, we are to experience God's *spiritual awakening* as never seen before. I believe that God granted my prayer by being part of this *awakening* because I asked. This book will be one way that mankind will finally acknowledge and believe in the one and only way to our coming together as a *collective force for mankind, and together we will be the ethical and moral conscience* through Jesus. Bless his holy name. Shalom. Amen.

Chapter Twenty-One

Angels

I WROTE ABOUT the *evil spirits*, so I wanted to let you know that the opposite are angels. As a former special education teacher, I worked with our *earthly* angels for twenty-six years. These angels are our children, and especially the children who choose to come to the earth to teach us lessons. First of all, we all are challenged in some way or another: emotionally, mentally, physically, and even spiritually. These children who are labeled as challenged are of the highest level of perfection from *heaven* among us. I saw compassion within each child, innocence within each little one, and the love Jesus bestowed upon each.

It was such an honor to be among these angels. On any given day at work, I felt so much better automatically just being around these children. They made my day important and worthwhile. I will be honest that there was a lot of paperwork, meetings, and more that was involved with this occupation. God bless all teachers, school employees, and church staff members, as well as private schoolteachers and employees. It is my personal opinion that teachers, police officers, and fire fighters should be paid more money rather than athletes. Why? A school may or may not provide a limit for spending per school year per teacher. As a former teacher, I usually spent close to $800.00 or $900.00, and maybe more some years, out of my own pocket because I wanted to do the best for the children under my care. Teachers see the need and spend their own money each year to pay for school supplies that a parent may not be able to supply in order for the student to have extra materials to enhance a particular lesson for that day, to store extra clothes and shoes if a child should have a bodily accident or get muddy while on the playground if and when the school clinic does not have the storage space nor sizes available, to give money if their lunch may have not been packed or was left at home or their school lunch account may have reached its limit and that day's meal is in question, to provide food for snack time, and to plan school holiday parties or special school events to make sure no child goes without treats or what is needed daily. There are so many details teachers are faced with concerning teaching lessons when a teacher may not be able to wait for a voucher to be approved, which may take days when a need is immediate. This is just a small glimpse into what teachers do for our children, and I wanted to voice just a few of these concerns that most teachers deal with on a daily basis because it is for the angels they teach. We do appreciate and thank you, teachers.

Parents, regular education teachers, family, friends, acquaintances, or anyone who knew or asked about my employment would usually make a comment such as, "You are such an angel to be able to do what you do!"

My response always was, "They are the angels. They give back so much more to me than what I could ever give to them!"

Jesus is of compassion. Jesus has such compassion for any of us who are challenged, sick, mentally ill, alcoholic, or addicted to drugs but do not display any mental, emotional, or physical abuse. We see through our earthly, natural eyes today. Jesus sees with his *spiritual* eyes. It is not just these angels' innocence or their patience Jesus sees and knows. It is so much more. They teach us to be more like Christ. They keep trying! Even with frustration with any given task presented or with any new or recently acquired skill or with any skill repeated over and over, these angels persist until a challenge is mastered. These angel children demonstrated to me that Jesus's heart is always with the souls who come to earth with such challenges because they choose to teach us God's *master lessons*.

There is more all of us need to do. It is the greatest commandment for us that we are to love our neighbors as ourselves. Not only are we to love at school or our place of work, but what about our home? What about our family and friends? What about our own neighborhood? What about our own community? What about our own state? What about the United States? What about the world we live?

Our children are our greatest assets. Be kind to them. Be gentle with them. Jesus so loved the little ones. Look at all children as *angels*. We were once those little ones at one time early in our own life. Children are God's creations. Children are creative. It is difficult to see an adult become disabled in any manner. It is heartbreaking when a child is born disabled or becomes disabled or challenged so young and endures hardships through life. I see Jesus through each child. I see the love that Jesus has for each child. There is a *heavenly* connection in the *spiritual* realm that is a mystery to us. There is less of that mystery between each child and Jesus. It is their innocence God loves. God gives each child who believes and knows rest through his peace and love beyond our adult comprehension. Amen.

Chapter Twenty-Two

Pray and Always Stand for Israel

THE BOOK OF Revelation has been on my mind frequently these days. There are so many interpretations of the last book of the Bible. I do not claim to understand that book nor claim to be a scholar. Because of my love for Israel as a child and as a Protestant, I just know the world must pray for and always stand for Israel, especially in the United States. We must never forget or desert Israel.

I will say that Jesus was born in Israel, his death took place in Israel, and his resurrection took place in Israel. As a Christian, that speaks volumes to me that Jesus will return to Israel, the home of his birth, to rule all nations in the final days. Israel was always on God's heart. Amen.

The "Women of the World in Prayer" in chapter 7 was given after 9/11, and *world* leaders are mentioned.

Also, I offer this prayer for Israel, the world, and world leaders by praying, "Abba Father, by faith and in the name of Jesus, hear our prayers for Israel, the world, and world leaders. We have learned that we do have access to you through Jesus and will ask through his holy name. Because we believe by faith in Jesus that his power and authority will protect Israel, peace will dominate this world God created and each world leader. The Spirit of God, our Creator, will lead each leader when it comes to their decision-making. Open the eyes and ears of all the world leaders not to have *hardened hearts.* We boldly ask out loud and with a bold and determined conviction as people of God's world to *collectively and consciously* unite through one heart through God's love. We denounce all *spirits of evil* that confront mankind. We do not claim or accept any confusion, division, strife, deception, trickery, guilt, condemnation, falsehood, or any *spiritual warfare.* We will stand against those attacks that denounce Jesus as not already victorious over 2,000 years ago.

Bless all of the military personnel and their families. If the world leaders had to fight on their own as individual leaders, Jesus, there would be no wars. Clean house, Lord, start at the very top and trickle on down to the bottom, so we will witness your *heavenly* paradise here on earth. You are the one who places leaders in power, and you are the one who dethrones these powerful men. In our days ahead, let us see who prays and stands for Israel. Our hearts, our prayers, and our love for Israel comes from you.

Bless Israel, the nations of the world, and the world leaders. Let us pray for *peace*! Thank you, Lord, for being the answer to this prayer. Amen."

Chapter Twenty-Three

I Am Not the Same on Any Given Day

IT IS IN our human nature to flip to the last chapter of any book we might be interested in, or we may possibly buy it as we read a glimpse of the summary and want to know the conclusion. We scour through to find the final synopsis, skim through the pages because the title got our attention, or just browse because of our curiosity. This is why I want these last few chapters to grab hold of you as a reader and for you to know *the answer*. This may be my one and only chance to let you know that this book is *not* about religion. No, in the year 2015, and in the years to come, this book's message is meant to inspire believers to rededicate their lives, to believe by the faith of Jesus, to speak the name of Jesus out loud, and to acknowledge who Jesus is to them personally.

I am not the same on any given day. Why? Even though I stand steadfast in my belief in Jesus, a Christian is to evolve to become Christlike on a deeper level each and every day. If I remain stagnant in my walk with Jesus from day to day, I am not growing as a follower of Christ. I did obey the calling from the *Spirit of God* to write this book for God's believers and God's nonbelievers, but how did I know that this book was inspired by the hand of God through me? It is because of a *knowing* that I would do this one day and the passion that was laid upon my heart by God. Each day I woke up the passion never left. As I am finishing this book, the cardinals have been seen through the large glass window first thing in the morning as I go to my computer to work. They have been for several weeks. Inwardly, I offer a silent prayer to God because I know this book's message is to revolutionize the way Christians and nonbelievers think today as we do renew our minds, hearts, spirits, souls, and our bodies daily. Why? God has been forgotten; we have forgotten God. Today, we do not think or consider the name of Jesus daily, and we do not think or consider who Jesus is to us daily. All along this has been the purpose for writing this book. This book is written to *glorify* the Father, the Son, and the Holy Spirit. Let us bless Jesus's holy name and know the Jesus that did walk upon the earth.

There is no way to get around being called a sinner. We are all sinners because we were born; it is as simple as that. In the reading, it does make a difference when you learn about the Old Law under the Old Covenant in the Old Testament. I do thank God to teach me more about the New Testament because we are no longer under the Old Law. We are now under God's *grace*, *mercy*, and *favor* daily.

What is *grace*? I saw the word "GRACE" in a mental vision. I wanted to learn more about this word. I am still learning. To me, *grace* is God's free and offered gift through the Gospel of Jesus Christ. Jesus is *grace*; the *grace* of Jesus is free and offered to us, which is sufficient daily. We are not able to earn it, buy it, or do good works for it or try to manipulate God to prove we deserve his *grace*. God is love. God loves you and me. God wants our best. Our *sinful nature* and sins do not cause God to withhold his *grace*. However, there are always consequences, so do not think I am saying that you may go ahead and continue any *sinful nature* all you want. No, when you acknowledge God and God's love, you will not want to do wrong. You will know and do what is the right choice to do. Why? You will not want to grieve the heart of God as you experience God's *grace*, God's *mercy*, and God's *favor*.

How am I able to not be the same person each day? I already know the answer. I go to Jesus when I have any negative thoughts. These negative thoughts want to keep me from focusing upon Jesus. These negative thoughts want to create fear within me, in order for me to think of and act in sin and to doubt God. This is where our own self-effort does the most damage. When we do have fear and worry this is when I have learned to rest in the Lord. Why? When we think we are definitely able to handle living life by our own self-effort, and when we do not value our self-worth as the children of God, we are guilty of that *sinful nature*.

Jesus is the answer. I do not question whether I was ever saved, whether I ever had my salvation, or whether I still do have my salvation. Once one has accepted Jesus and becomes a believer, there is nothing you or I will ever do to lose our salvation! Did you truly accept Jesus as your savior? Jesus paid the price once and for *all* for *all* mankind. It is done! If not, I offer this invitation for you to rededicate yourself to Jesus. It is in knowing you do not have to worry about your salvation. You do not want to think about sins or sinning by means of any *sinful nature*, and you do not have to live life without God's help. You do not have to do anything but accept Jesus who is righteous, and know you are made righteous by believing by the faith of Jesus. Learn more from reading God's words and God's promises in the Bible daily.

Jesus is the one and only one who does bestow his increase and his abundance in your life and in my life. Don't you want to receive these freely offered gifts? God is waiting for us to ask through prayer. God does bless us on a daily basis. God's love is endless. God wants to bless us as his children. I use to wonder and feel guilty and think it was selfish to ask for blessings for myself. No, I ask God to bless my family, friends, and any person I come into contact with during my day or on anyone's birthday or for special occasions, and I think about being more observant to look for the many blessings every moment of each day. Why? God blesses us, so we are able to be a blessing to others. How could I be the same on any given day when I experience so much? Because I love Jesus.

The words of knowledge I have received over the last forty-plus years are my many master lessons, as well, and are repeated in some of the chapters. Why? Each one needs to be ingrained within your mind, your heart, your spirit, your soul, and your body. The only way to do this is for me to repeat the *master lessons*, so you hear these *master lessons* over and over until you live and breathe each as the life force within you as a believer and Christian. I do invite all believers to rededicate themselves and to stand for Jesus and stand steadfast by the faith of Jesus in 2015 and in the years to come, especially for our children and for our grandchildren. I invite all nonbelievers to consider Jesus, to accept Jesus, and to know God's love. When you think of each lesson you learn daily, these *master lessons* will become your way of life *by the faith of Jesus* who does live within you and does live within me.

How could I be the same on any given day when I do believe Jesus will pour out his *Spirit* as mankind unites our voices together as one to speak against the *spirits of evil* and as we acknowledge the power of God's love? Love will be at the core of our *collective and ethical conscience concerning the morals of all mankind.* Why? The name of Jesus will be acknowledged in the year 2015 and in the years to come. All will speak the name of Jesus and the word "love." Together, each of us will know and speak the name of Jesus, which is this book's message that I write about as I end this book. Collective conscience is not a term I made up, it is another word of knowledge given by the *Spirit of God,* which I could not ignore or omit. This is our eternal *master lesson.* Jesus is the one and only one who could do what God required of him. Jesus is our answer.

The United States and the world are not to ignore the name of the Father, the Son, and the Holy Spirit as we do today. Let us evolve daily to be made in the likeness of Jesus Christ. The evolving comes only through the *Spirit of God if* and *when* we do dare to *hope,* to believe, to trust, to desire, and to seek God daily and not just on Sundays. It is within our heart and within our spirit where we find the true essence of God. I call it our *spirit heart.* I walked away from religion and walked toward believing in our living and our loving God. I vowed to myself that I would not give up as I asked these questions as a child, as a teenager, and as a young adult.

"Where are you, God? Where? I do not know where to find you in this world today?

You be my teacher, you, Jesus. You teach me," was my frequent inner and spoken prayer.

These were my frequent questions. I was about to be *awakened* by the *Spirit of God* in a way I only felt when I first joined the church as a child. This *awakening* was different. As I became an adult, the *Spirit of God* became my *Master Teacher*. Shalom. Amen.

We do need to remember that the Old Testament consisted of too many laws; it was the Old Law of the Old Covenant and included the Ten Commandments. Like most of us, as a child I watched the movie called *The Ten Commandments* and other religious movies as well. I wondered how anyone could keep all ten of the commandments. If any person could *not* keep all ten, we were in trouble as a society. People do not feel as though they could ever measure up to those Godly standards. People still live by and quote them today. People honestly still try to keep the commandments as we have been taught through religion. When I mentioned evolving daily, I do believe the Ten Commandments are holy, God-given, and moral laws through the old laws of the Old Covenant as read in the Old Testament. I believe that the Old Testament is the foreshadowing of God's divine plan and the pending prophecy of the birth of Jesus. People did not know what sin was then; they lived under the Old Law of the Old Covenant. Jesus did as God required. By the faith of Jesus we are saved once and for all time. The *Spirit of God* teaches that we are no longer under that Old Law of the Old Covenant. Yes, I believe it will be hard for people to grasp and understand this *master lesson*. It was hard for me for the longest time to renew my mind because I wanted to hold on for dear life to the religious teachings of my childhood. I try not to think of, and try to refrain from, the teachings concerning the Old Law of the Old Covenant I grew up learning. Again, I did struggle with this *master lesson*. It was hard to forsake these childhood beliefs. Please, do not get me wrong by thinking I would ever disregard God's moral laws as unholy! I would *never* dismiss what is holy to God. I would *not* want to grieve the heart of God by deliberately thinking of sin or sinning, which is our *sinful nature*. Jesus paid a hefty price to save all of mankind.

The New Covenant did reveal our *sinful nature* that we know as our sins or as us sinning. I do believe and do accept the New Covenant *by the faith of Jesus*. It is important that we do pay attention to the preposition used in the last sentence. I had usually used the phrase "through the faith of Jesus" as I had heard in the church. *Through the faith of Jesus* may seem to mean about the same when you hear the phrase "by the faith of Jesus." *Through the faith of Jesus* was taught to me in church as it does relate to the sacrifice Jesus paid for us, his suffering for all mankind once and for all on the *cross*, and the blood of Christ that Jesus shed for you and me. What is vital and important through the *master lesson* to acknowledge and to know is that it was *only* "by the faith of Jesus" that Jesus did indeed have faith and did obey God. That was God's divine destiny finished once and for all and could only be accomplished *by the faith of Jesus*. That is so important for believers of today too. Think how dramatic this phrase becomes when we do grasp the realization that it is *by the faith of Jesus* that Jesus knew he was the only one God chose. Jesus was whom God sent to fulfill all biblical prophecies. The name of Jesus and who Jesus is has been greatly diminished today. I do believe and do accept the New Covenant. *By the faith of Jesus,* I know *all* of my past sins, present sins, and future *sins* are paid in full for all eternity. It was not about us; it is about what Jesus did for us.

Under the New Covenant, believers and nonbelievers may think this gives anyone and everyone the okay to sin, *miss all the marks,* and to continue their *sinful nature* as one pleases twenty-four hours of each and every day. Why? You think you have now been given permission to sin? You think you will get away with sin? You think God has already forgiven you anyway, so why not sin? When one knows Jesus and has a loving, cherished, and personal relationship with Christ, they will not want to think of sinning, *miss any mark,* or hold onto that *sinful nature* as a human being. Mankind has always had that *sinful nature* within us, which is why we need Jesus! Christ knew we would not be able to keep all of the commandments. Originally, in the Old Testament, God gave the old laws because he needed to show us our *sinful nature* and what sinning was to us as his children.

I am not the same on any given day because God is love, and God loves us. As you become a believer through Christ, you need to hear repeatedly and often that God loves you. I repeat to myself that God loves me whenever I need to feel someone cares for me.

I am elevated to a higher level that connects to God within my heart. You need to believe often in God's mysterious and mighty power that is indeed supernatural. When I mentioned evolving each day, I do know that the love of God, *the Spirit of God,* and his strength gives me my inner joy I felt had been lacking within me, which I seemed to be missing on my own. Joy is doing what you know God wants you to do. Is it a sin not to do what you know is the right choice.

Who is able to be the same on any given day when you know that your righteous believing leads to your righteous behaving? I always believed in natural opposites. I pay attention to the lessons one learns through the opposite effects.

<u>An example</u>: You may choose to yell at a person when aggravated, or you might remain calm. You may go to God in prayerful meditation and not rely totally upon your self-effort to be able to change your learned behavior. It may not be the other person who needs to change. God will change your attitude and you from within.

<u>Another example</u>: You may choose to gossip about someone, or you can choose to pray for that person who has mistreated you or who you perceive to be your enemy. Let us learn to pray for our enemies, and let us ask God to avenge the wrong on our behalf, which is in God's hands anyway.

When I use the phrase "collective consciousness," I am addressing the *heart of all mankind* as I refer to the *spiritual heart* within all men, women, and children. God's words and God's promises are his truth, which is the only way mankind will transform. God is the only one who will awaken our *spirit hearts*; we are a prideful people and nation. My prayer as a Granny and prayer warrior is that the *Spirit of God* will pour out his Holy Spirit upon all of us. People are suffering, and I ask God to make his love known to this generation and our children's generations to come. We have lost *hope* because of today's manmade and natural disasters, school and random shootings, our inefficient government, and so much more. God is in control. Let us turn back to God, especially now, so we know the creator of the universe. May our *conscience* be stronger in our belief *by the faith of Jesus.* God wants to love us. Let us love Christ, accept his love, and speak to *glorify* his holy name. When you accept God's love, you will accept God's love within yourself straight to your *spirit heart* with no doubt. God and his love will be the power you will live by and not the human flesh of the *sinful nature* that will be ever present with every conflict. Be a witness for Christ in today's world. Give God the *praise he deserves* by talking to our beloved creator. May we in our *conscience* give more of our praise and gratitude to God. Shalom. Amen.

You will never be the same on any given day when you talk to God. God is a friend to love and trust. It is normal to ask who, what, where, why, when, how, and more as a human in the flesh. Here are a few questions I asked as a young child:

> "Are you real from the Bible stories?"
> "Where are you?"
> "Make yourself known to me!"
> "When will you show up in my life?"
> "Are you real to others and not me?"
> "Why don't I hear from you?"
> "What do I need to do to know you?"
> "Who are you really?"
> "How do you love me after all that I have done?"

Here are a few examples of my communications as an adult as I speak to the Father, Son, and Holy Spirit:

> "Good morning, my sweet Lord."
> "Thank you, God, for sharing your beauty with me."
> "Please, protect me as I run my errands on the road today."
> "Help me hand over this problem through your will and your solution."
> "Sorry, I should have let that car out in front of me and waited."
> "I love you. Wow, you love us more than I will ever comprehend."

God hears all questions and comments; there is nothing he does not know about you. God hears our words of thanksgiving, gratitude, and praise. God wants to hear from us on a daily basis. He is as close as your next breath. Read the Bible, his holy words. Talk to God as you would to someone you love and trust as a friend. God wants you to be sincere when you talk to him. He is friend with a sense of humor as well. Prayers are times to be truly heartfelt with your talks with God as your best friend. Prayers do not have to be in a different tone of your voice, which is not natural. Be yourself as you communicate with God.

As I pull weeds in my yard, I joke with God about why he had to create weeds. In my spirit, I know weeds protect the soil when land is barren. I ask another question about large, black crows eating the grass seed just sowed. I feel so close to God when I am around nature and see beauty grow. God is that seed of love within us. We grow and bloom through his love. Shalom. Amen.

Nature and music are pleasing to God. Along with renewing your mind each and every day, the renewing and attitude of the *spirit heart* is important to God. A pure heart is vital. God knows you better than you will ever know yourself. You will never be able to fool God. You might as well just tell God the truth about you. He already knows our faults, *all* of them. By being open and honest, God will lighten the load. Think how prideful we are when we do not trust God enough to say to God that we are handing *all* cares to him. When you finally come to the end of your rope, so to speak, that is what it is like to surrender *all* to him. In my earlier days when I was trying to learn this concept, I wrote down my worries on a piece of paper, placed the note in an envelope, and dropped the paper in a trashcan at the mall or wherever I happened to be, as a symbol that I was letting go and giving it to God to handle for me. I would sometimes visualize laying it in a box at the foot of the *cross*. I learned that I had to give it *all* to God. Laying anything and everything at the *cross* is what I say and do today. In my *spirit heart*, I know that God even hears my silent prayers offered to him in love from within my heart that understands the sacredness and reverence of who God is to me. I know his love from and through my *spirit heart*. You will be governed by the Holy Spirit and not from the human flesh of the *sinful nature*. It is God who lifts us up more than we will ever know. Because of my love for Christ, I would not ever want to grieve the heart of God. He will teach you, cleanse you, rebuke you, and love you.

I am still learning how awesome it is to be loved by God. I used to say to God that my love does not seem adequate to offer it to him because I am a human being in the flesh, even though I know God is within me. Now, I know that is an insult and a sin to say that my love is inadequate. God is within me, and I am within God. We are one. I am righteous through the righteousness of Jesus. Nothing will separate me from God or God's love from me. There will be tests and trials in life on this *earth*. God walks with me through this life. God is in the midst of all of my daily circumstances and ready to be my helper and comforter.

It is my prayer that our nation and world evolves to the point that we acknowledge God more today and that we believe in Jesus, *the cross*, and in the blood of Jesus. We do accept, claim, and proclaim that the *Spirit of God* is alive in today's world, rather than the arrogance and pride through our human *sinful nature*. Pray to God as your friend during your talks to God, and pray for all of our *spirit hearts* to be softened and *not hardened* toward our God. None of us will ever be the same on any given day! Shalom. Amen.

Chapter Twenty-Four

Jesus is *The Answer*

IN SUMMARIZING MY book, Jesus is *the answer*. Jesus did obey the will of God for you and for me. You and I will stand with Jesus because we believe Jesus is the *one and only* sacrifice, our Messiah that came to save mankind from all of our *sinful nature* as *no one else* could. As *one* within the Trinity, God chose to come to the earth in human flesh in man's image that God created. Jesus was born of the Virgin Mary. It is *by the faith of Jesus* that we know these truths. Jesus died on the *cross* and was resurrected on the third day. This is Christianity!

For me, I do want to surround myself with anyone who *genuinely cares and loves me*. The answer is Jesus because our loved ones at times do fail us. We fail our loved ones as well. I look to Jesus, and Jesus is where I focus my trust daily. We were given life, but we believe it is because we gave our life to Jesus that we are saved. No, that is what we have heard and been taught. *Jesus gave us life* and is our life, our strength, and our might, and it is not by our own effort by any means as humans. Think about this: Over 2,000 years ago we were not born. Jesus knew each of us. He knew our own personal *sinful nature* beforehand and our sufferings to come. Jesus went to the *cross* as the *one and only* acceptable sacrifice on our behalf. When reading God's words and reading God's promises, we evolve to believe in Jesus. Our believing in Jesus leads us to become Christlike, and we become righteous because Jesus is righteous. We become righteous *by the faith of Jesus.* Our righteousness is 100% established and sealed for eternity within the Trinity: the Father, the Son, and the Holy Spirit. Because Jesus obeyed God, and because of what Jesus did for us, we will never fully understand God's sacrifice of the Son of God. In prayer, I say thank you, God, thank you!

With age and experience, the wisdom I offer is our *original* response to accepting Jesus. By the faith of Jesus we are corresponding to our *initial* belief in Jesus. It is the way we respond to everything else from then on that shows our obedience to Christ. There is no way to keep my tally to see if I ever measure up to any obedience on my part. How would I ever know? This made me think more about Jesus's obedience to the Father. *By the faith of Jesus* is our key to manifestations happening. Once you wholeheartedly know this truth, you will tap into the many blessings that God is waiting to grant and bestow upon you because of God's love. Do not ever forget that Jesus is the answer; it is that Jesus obeyed God. It is because of Jesus's obedience I owe *my all* to Jesus. I am nothing without Jesus. That is not a negative self-comment. It is my truth. Is it your truth? What would we be without Jesus? Who would we be without our Christ? When I thought of the *cross,* I usually had tears in my eyes. Now, I have tears of joy because I know how precious Jesus is to me. Jesus did what no other person could do: Jesus fulfilled God's will to save you and me from the *spiritual warfare* in this world and to acknowledge all of us are under God's care daily. When I was younger, I held on to the truth of the Biblical story of Easter and Jesus's *obedience to the Father*! The obedience of Jesus is why Jesus is the answer. The Bible foretold of God's divine plan to hold us in the palm of his hands. Jesus is victorious. Jesus does sit down at the right hand of God. *It is finished. It is done.*

What you believe will convict you to behave accordingly to God's will. One who does believe in *righteous believing* will live their life through corresponding by *righteous behavior.* Doesn't this thought make sense? Our righteousness does not mean that God looks the other way or gives us a free pass to sin due to our *sinful nature.* There are natural and lawful consequences to our *sinful nature,* so you should be aware that you are responsible for the choices you make. Righteousness convicts us to not want to behave or participate in any *sinful nature* or ponder about sin or sinning before God. We do not want our *sinful nature* or thoughts of sin or our actual sinning or misbehaviors to grieve God. Yes, over the generations God's people did grieve God's heart. God has taken a lot of grief from mankind. God is omnipotent and is able to love us unconditionally no matter what. With one breath from God our life could end, and God's will is done at his appointed and due time. When people do not consider that their behavior grieves God, what kind of people are we? Have we become so arrogant and apathetic toward God that we do not care about God anymore? Do we look at the Bible as an obsolete book about Christianity? Look at the businesses open on Sundays. Look at the businesses closed on Sundays. We have forgotten that the Sabbath is God's holy day. I try not to shop on Sunday unless there is a real emergency.

A *master lesson* is that we never lose our righteousness. When we do not believe in our own righteousness *by the faith of Jesus* we *fall from grace.* To *fall from grace* simply means that you may move away from God for that split second when you doubt God. You are still righteous. You just forgot for that split second that God is righteous, and so are you. That also means we now have to become aware that we have a *hardened heart* when Jesus is not considered or thought about with every moment-by-moment decision we make in life. Jesus desired to partake in your life and in my life. Please, do not deny Jesus. Please, let us partake with Jesus.

As humans, we do not always ask God to lead us or help us make our choices or teach us to act Christlike in our daily walk through Jesus. As a reminder, humans just will not let it be or let it go concerning a problem or situation without thinking we need to do something to fix what needs to be repaired. This is where our self-effort cancels out what Jesus will do. God understands our human frailties and extends his *grace, mercy, and favor* each day. Think about this truth throughout your day and look for his *grace, mercy,* and *favor.* Do rest in the Lord. Do wait patiently.

Our righteousness is trying to be stolen from us mentally by *spiritual warfare* and the unseen *spirits of evil*. Please, read the chapter titled "Evil in God's World" also. God is on our side and is protecting us. God does not get any pleasure from seeing evil come upon his children. God wants his very best for you and me. However, the *spirits of evil* will try to attack believers in Jesus, but they will not succeed. Because we know and belong to Jesus, the devil trembles! By the name of Jesus and *by the faith of Jesus*, we are victorious through Jesus. Jesus is our strength and might to overcome. Do not listen to these *spirits of evil* when we are weak, sick, have a disease, are poverty stricken, are surrounded by crime, become part of natural or manmade disasters, feel depressed or lonely, are victims of hatefulness, sense hopeless, are vulnerable, are in despair, see racial or ethnic prejudices, witness economic difficulties, or anything else that we acknowledge to be the *spirits of evil* and not of God. Again and again, do be vigilant in prayer through Jesus to be guarded against anyone or anything that tries to bring division within your family and home, your neighborhood, your community, your city, your state, your nation, and your world. *Spiritual warfare* and *spirits of evil* are real and will try to bring division, strife, and unrest, and the mind is where the damage starts and invades.

Because of the recent police encounters with the public in 2014 and 2015, this bears repeating over and over. Why do people think they are entitled to destroy or burn a business or vandalize or cause damage to someone's property? Why is it that you, as one person, would not think to do that when alone? Yet, when in a group of people you think it is okay because everyone else is doing it? Think about what you would really do as an individual in any given situation. Then, do not use the excuse to burn or destroy within a group. Please, think before you do any of this, whether it is a riot, protest, or other rallies that Americans may face in the future.

The two words "collective," *as all of us together*, and "conscience," *as all of us living with ethics and morals through Jesus*, have stayed with me as a knowing throughout writing this book. These two words are important words to God. I believe this to be our greatest gift to God. God does not need any gift from us. Though, wouldn't it be nice not to grieve the heart of God as our gift to him anyway? The Deceiver and the *spirits of evil* are on the rampage for *spiritual warfare*, ready to try to destroy Jesus and us. The Power of the Air thinks he is one of royalty and one of intelligence. Let us demand and command the *spirits of evil* to know their time is running out and limited because we Christians are ready and standing as a *collective*, as well as a *conscience*, group for Christ. Are you ready? Are we? As this *collective* group of people remains conscience as believers for Christ, it is in our thinking that we acknowledge Jesus as the one and only ultimate judge of our moral ethics upon our final judgment before God and that of Judgment Day. That will be the day when there will be God's review of our lives and his execution of judgment done in a loving way with clarity. God's judgment prevails and not the evil plans to defeat Christians. We are to be *conscience* of Jesus, the *cross*, Jesus's blood, and his righteousness, especially Jesus's obedience to the Father. We are to obey Jesus and do so when we believe, trust, and have faith in our Lord.

Are you ready to stand for Jesus no matter what the circumstance or situation? Be proud to call yourself a Christian and to be known as a Christian. God does know what each day will bring and will prepare us for that day. Have you really prepared to know God? When a believer or nonbeliever does prepare to know God, God makes his preparation and path known to you. God is waiting for this generation to ask him into their lives once again. This is your invitation. God is waiting to hear your spoken declaration. With God's heartfelt invitation, God's love is freely offered. God teaches and convicts us through his loving presence so that we become more Christlike every step of our walk through him. You will stumble on the way as a human being, but God is there to pick you up each time. Because you will learn that God knew you before you were even born, you can surrender your life into his hands. Why not surrender to our creator? Why not join and become one through Jesus as a united front of believers who do not like division or strife, which is another Biblical word for no peace. Our *collective consciousness* depends upon God and his love. What are we to do with love, our love? Love Jesus. Love your enemies. Jesus is the answer!

Now, in prayer, you know to ask Jesus for what you need. As a believer, you were *made* a partaker through Jesus and did not just become a partaker by your own self-effort. Be bold and be a partaker. How? You are *made* a partaker when you understand God's words and promises and speak out loud with your mouth that you believe. I believe that the *Spirit of God* is the breath of God and neither is separate to me.

If and *when* God is not the priority in our life, expect God to delay his manifestations, even if we may pray in the name of Jesus. A lesson we all need to be mindful of is that we need to learn not to complain, moan, groan, or speak any defeating words daily. Yes, I am reminded of this *master lesson* as well. In 2015, I will talk to God as I have learned another *master lesson* as this book is finished. In prayer, I will ask to be *made* to partake in manifestations, and it might be one of deliverance that I need for that day and moment by moment. I will pray and thank God to *see* manifestations in my physical world day after day with gratitude and praise. Whether I see it manifested in my physical world that day or not, I will believe the manifestation is on the verge of eventually becoming seen in my physical world. The answer for what I need through prayer is in God's storehouse from God's unseen kingdom, which supplies *all* my needs with abundance and increase. The manifestations will be on God's timetable and according to God's will.

Jesus came for us to know our Father who is his Father. I also invite you to know *by the faith of Jesus* who Jesus is and of his power when we speak the name of Jesus. Jesus is the Son of God. Jesus, the breath and *spirit of God*, is of the Father. Jesus wants you to know the answer. The *Master Teacher* will help you to understand the words of God as you read the Bible. The Bible is the inspired words of God; it is the same Bible yesterday, today, and tomorrow. Shalom. Amen.

This Granny prays with united Christians, "Father, the book is about finished. Thank you for the many lessons taught to me, *Master Teacher*. *By the faith of Jesus*, I will continue to evolve. Jesus, you walked the earth going about your business, yet you stopped and turned to work your miracles for whoever needed you at that moment. You acknowledged the *spirits of evil* and spoke out loud to the different ones according to each person and what possessed that person. *By the faith of Jesus* I ask parents and grandparents to boldly agree and pray with me for God's protection, especially for our children and our grandchildren who are the targets of unspeakable *evil spirits* in our world today. We will say out loud and with firm conviction that there is no room or place here for the *spirits of evil*. We stand against any more pain directed toward all of your young children and young adults and the more mature that inhabit your world. In your name, Jesus, we ask you, Father, to hear our prayers to eliminate fears, sufferings, abuses, and terrorism. It is *by the faith of Jesus* that it is done! Therefore, we command and demand the *spirits of evil* to be stomped out and that negative thoughts within our minds, hearts, spirits, souls, and bodies are demolished, crushed, pulverized, gone forever, rebuked, banned, and cast out as demonstrated through your Biblical miracles. Will us to be your agents of change. You are our agent for change. Jesus, we acknowledge that you are the answer, our one and only answer. Shalom. Amen."

It is January 3, 2015, and I saw the yard full of orioles as I opened my door, ready to go get my morning newspaper. They stood still as I saw more in the road, across the street, and to the right in my neighbor's direction. The yard was full of orioles as first seen around two weeks before 9/11 at our previous residence. The second time I saw so many orioles was around two weeks before an uncle died, which seems strange because the birds were in the backyard near the pool at our new home during a light winter snow. The third time I saw the orioles is described earlier in the book when a friend's grandchild's pending death was sensed. I stood at the door in prayer, asking that *I hoped* it was not another 9/11 to come. I have learned to ask for very specific and very detailed words of knowledge now. Whatever I sensed might come immediately or within a two-week time frame. Anyway, I emailed my oldest brother, my editor, and my manager to tell them about the orioles. *If* and *when* a person or something comes to mind and lingers, I will go before God to verify that the word of knowledge is from God. At this moment, at 10:40 in the morning, I have no idea what to expect. I will wait and rest in God right now. I had turned on the television numerous times to CNN, and the special with

Anthony Bourdain: Parts Unknown about his visit to Paris was on repeatedly. He has done a lot of traveling shows in different countries, and I wondered why it was Paris and not another city. I wonder if this was my answer to seeing the orioles before the terrorists attack in Paris.

I have seen cardinals every day for the last three to four weeks as I finish this book. They are close to the glass room where I am typing on my computer. God sent them for me to know that my prayers have been heard, the prayers concerning writing this book. The cardinals sent by God are given to me as comfort. When I see the cardinals, God is so near. God is forever present.

In 2015, let us open our renewed minds, hearts, spirits, souls, and bodies to acknowledge we need Jesus. We do humbly ask for your blessings.

This Granny prays, "We surrender our all to you this day as the nation called the United States of America and as the inhabitants of your world. Shalom. Amen."

Chapter Twenty-Five

Consider These Questions and Answers

I AM NO expert on knowing how to prayer correctly, but I wonder if this is why people are reluctant to pray. I talk to God as a friend who listens to me because I know God is interested in my life. Whenever I think of something or someone, I automatically go to God in prayer because God already knows what is on my mind. Why not go ahead and discuss the situation, circumstance, and problem with God? Why not do the same when it concerns a person or people you think about as well? I do try to remember to address God as *Father* in prayer. Asking for what we need is the key because so many times we do not ask! If you do not ask, you will not receive so learn to ask specifically and in detail, which was a *master lesson* learned. Remember to thank Jesus, remember to praise the name of Jesus and who Jesus is to you and to show gratitude daily for all your blessings great and small. When I catch myself thinking or saying out loud a complaint, I try to turn a negative into a positive. An example may be that I am not able to move and get out of bed.

I pray, "Good morning, God. Thank you for my arms and legs and for this comfortable bed. Let's get moving! *All* is well. You make me whole."

These sections were written as part of the chapter "Delight Yourself in the Lord" originally. However, I was just gently inspired by God to offer this book as an invitation to believers and nonbelievers. I was again gently inspired by God to share some of my personal prayers to God. I try not to repeat the same words over and over in prayer to God, even though I know God is patient and loving. My repetition seems to show my doubt in who Jesus is to me. Learn the different names given to Jesus and God in the Bible and use them in prayer. I may use the word "shalom," along with "amen," as I close because it is the Jewish word for peace. Why? Shalom was laid upon my heart because of Israel. I am comfortable using it in prayers.

I rest in the Lord.

Question : Have you learned to rest in the Lord?

<u>Here is my prayerful meditation</u>: I pray, "Father, I do not want to hold on to any control anymore. My prayer is one of surrender *by the faith of Jesus.* Surrender is not being passive or not caring about what happens throughout my daily life, but I will rest daily through you, Lord. By trusting that no matter what trial or test comes my way, you need me to step aside. *Heavenly* Father, I know that you are already working on my behalf. However, I may not like the trial or test; I just know it is the way I respond to that test or trial that gets your attention, God. Whatever trial or test, God, you are with me. I will wait on you, Lord, because I believe you see and know *all.* Your power lifts me up, and *hope* is always present. Jesus, you are meek, but you are not weak. You always took your time to heal and to minister to your beloved earthly children through your well-designed and divine destiny. Thank you for revealing yourself to me in my due season. Jesus, you have demonstrated your supernatural presence and power where your love is needed through my life. You are so needed in today's world. Resting in you is a lesson I will need to remember, especially when I am saddened to see and hear about bad things happening in the world. I will remember you are always in control. You are in control of the economy. You are in control of the governments. You are in control of the weather. You are in the midst and in control of lovingly adopting aborted babies to be with you in *heaven.* You are in control of *all* human rights and freedom. You are in control of extending

your love through us and extending our love to others. Yes, I will stand on your holy word that marriage is between one man and one woman. The same-sex partners and lives of those in marriages are between you and that couple. You are in the midst and in control of human suffering. Because I surrender my life through you, Lord, I will not fear. I behold you, your love, and your will that protects and comforts me. *By the faith of Jesus*, I am well. I am whole. My prayer is that the United States and the world behold you, God. You know that has been my desire and in my prayers for years. I ask you, *Spirit of God*, pour your love upon our nation and *your* world. We will seek you, God, in the midst of everything. In your name, Jesus, thank you for loving us. Teach and show us that your love is the answer. You and you alone change the hearts of mankind. Teach us to pray for our enemies that terrorize the world because we do not understand that hate. Shalom. Amen."

You must bare it all to God.

Question : Are you hiding from God, and what are you hiding from God?

<u>Here is my prayerful meditation</u>: I pray, "Lord, I do not cover up or hide my *spirit heart* from you. I come to you and speak to you, my friend. I know that *I* am important in your eyes. Today, *I* come before you believing in my self-worth through you and not my self-absorbing, self-centered, and selfish human ego. I come before you with a pure heart. Cleanse me and clarify your wisdom of knowledge to my *conscience* through your holy thoughts, holy words, holy promises, and holy will. You know I am human and not perfect. I do come before you, the Almighty I Am, to your very holy place. That holy place is through you. You dwell within me. I am holy through you, God. As a believer, I want everyone to know that I am blessed to know you and that everything is holy in your eyes. Some may not realize that, but you teach them, Lord. When I come before you I begin to know who I am through you, Christ. I come to your holy place. When I rest in you, Lord, I am before your presence with you and your holiness. It is your holy place of renewal where everything is renewed. I come to

you, my sweet Lord, with all details, small and large. You hear my prayers and are working on my behalf whether I see or feel it or not. I do accept whatever cleansing or chastising from you, Father, *if* and *when* I am impatient and interfere due to my self-effort. My prayers are offered with a heartfelt apology if any prayer resembles treating you as a genie that grants wishes on demand. I want to come before you asking for your help and depending upon you to provide only what I need to be content, not for what I always immediately want. Thank you that you provide unexpectedly beyond my expectations when my desires match up with your desires for me. My will must connect with your will in all matters. I come before you, God, with any evil thoughts, my *sinful nature, missing the mark*, any negativity that invades my mind, or when I feel the devil is whispering doubtful thoughts within my mind. I ask that I be governed and led by your *spirit*, God, rather than by my human flesh. I am not perfect and never will be except through you, Christ. I bare my life and *all* life secrets before you. There is nothing I want to hide from you. I may be ashamed about what I have thought, said, or done. However, when I honestly confess and come clean I still feel accepted and loved very much through your eyes. You love me. I do come clean before you. Therefore, I am not ashamed now because I know you always love me. You know me better than I will ever know myself. You are almighty God, the holy and all knowing God of *all* life. Thank you. I ask in your name, Jesus. Shalom. Amen."

Here again, I use the word "I" not to build my ego as some psychologists may assume. The word "I" sometimes means that in our culture. We do not value ourselves or feel worthy as humans, and we feel as though we might not measure up. *The Spirit of God* taught me the ultimate value of being a child of his is to always feel worthy and to know the reverence and sacredness of the word "I." You and *I* are important to God. Because of God, *I* know *I* am righteous through God.

My beloved, it is finished.
You are beloved by God.
We are God's beloved.

Question : Did you know it is finished from that holy Easter
of all Easter Sundays?

Here is my prayerful meditation: I pray, "Thank you, Father,
that all our *sins* are forgiven. You so loved the world, Christ,
that you bore *all* of our sins once and for all. We are so beloved
by you. It is hard for some people to believe, accept, and claim.
We do not always believe, accept, and claim your unconditional
love. Why? Your love has amazed me through your words and
promises for *all* time. Each time I think of your life, Jesus, I am
amazed as I read the Bible. When I think of your relationship
with your disciples, I am amazed by these relationships. When
I think of your healings, I am amazed by your power and the
power to heal through God, Jesus. We are beloved. Our *sinful
nature,* or what I call *missing the mark,* was and is finished at
the *cross.* Because of that Easter Sunday, our *missing the mark*
is finished through your love. Because of the *cross,* you so loved
us. Because of your blood, you suffered in our place because
you loved mankind and me. Because of you, the *cross,* and your
blood, I would not want to deliberately *miss the mark* by not
learning from any of my mistakes. I would not want to grieve
you, Father, Son, and Holy Ghost. This does not ever give me
permission to ponder about my *sinful nature* or think that it
gives me license to do whatever I want to do. I will never try to get
away with any *sinful nature.* I am under the New Covenant and
am forgiven for *missing all my marks.* After reading about the
Old Testament, my mind, *spirit heart,* soul, and physical body
are once again radically renewed as I read the New Testament
today. I know that you are a patient God. Let me always *fathom*
the depth of love through your love. Let me always *fathom* the
breath of love through your love. There is so much more about
you and your love that is not revealed to us as humans. I am not
able to fully *fathom* the depth of your love as a human being,
which does not exist beyond human comprehension. You died for
me despite my *missing the marks.* My so-called *sinful nature*
is not part of you. *Spirit of God,* you are where *all* is finished on
the *cross.* My life through you, Christ, began the day you made
yourself known to me because I believed *by the faith of Jesus.* I

am a Christian in my belief and by my faith through you. God, you are faithful and everlasting in your words and promises. Thank you for sending your beloved son, the one and only one, to die for our sins and offering him for our salvation. Thank you, Prince of Peace. Shalom. Amen."

Question any word or words of knowledge.

Question : Have you received any word(s) of knowledge through God?

Here is my prayerful meditation: I pray, "Father, thank you for your *spiritual gift* I have received. I accept and claim each word of knowledge as I come before you in prayer to discern whether this word of knowledge is from you or from the *spirits of evils*. Protect me and guide me with your truth, love, and light. Thank you, Son of God. Shalom. Amen."

God brings a balanced life.
God walks with you.
God is not frivolous.
God is a priority and vital.

Question : Are you a content person and a person who knows peace?

Here is my prayerful meditation: I pray, "Lord, you alone are what brings satisfaction and balance to my life, it is not school, work, daily events, or people. We do fill our time due to our human feelings that cause emptiness, so take away anything that is not pleasing to you. If we are not valuing you and putting you first in our lives, show us that contentment and peace is through you only. You do quench our thirst, curve any hunger, decrease cravings, withdraw addictions, calm anxieties, love through loneliness, change immoral or sexual desires to your moral standards, give knowledge to who you are as we try to fill our dissatisfaction, curtail explorations or various hobbies that do not complete us, reduce buying and using the latest electronic equipments we think we have to have, omit wasted free or leisure time watching too many movies or television programs, limit playing different sports all year round due to physical exhaustion, prevent searching for pornography that destroys one's dignity and family values, stop any form of gambling, find one who is at the end of their rope due to frustration and sees no way out to any problem or situation, and delete every negative thought another human or I have experienced and will experience through life. That is why I know you are the answer every second of every day. I need you. I need your help! We need your help! I do appreciate you. What would I do without you, Immanuel? Shalom. Amen."

Motives are why do we do what we do.
What are you addicted to now, why not Christ?

Question : What is so important that motivates you more than Jesus?

Here is my prayerful meditation: I pray, "I do face that at times I am self-centered because I am human. My focus is not always upon you, Jesus, as it should be. I do ask myself what I do regularly and what interests me? I do ask myself whether what interests me is in line with what you would have me do; what would Jesus do? I do question myself often about how you fit into my daily schedule and whether or not what I do pleases you. Why do we do what we do? There is no fooling you! Things of this world will fade, corrode, die, vanish, lose value, be destroyed, and not fulfill me. What I really treasure in my life is evident to you. There my *spirit heart* will be also. Help me keep my focus on you as number one in my life. People, wealth, health, fads, and everything will wilt and fail. You will be *breaking the ground*, taking my *hands off the wheel*, and *running the car into the ditch* so to speak. God, you are eternal! Each and every time you may use a difficult circumstance to build my closeness to you. I will look for the moments before, during, and after every storm in life to witness your strength as you *take the wheel* when I need you to steer me in your direction as I get off course periodically. Thank you, King of Kings. I need you and your help daily! Shalom. Amen."

Just come and worship; leave the distractions.

Question : Do you worship God in many ways?

Here is my prayerful meditation: "God, I am taking time to talk to you here while standing at my kitchen sink. I was thinking of you while driving to do errands earlier this morning. I was paying attention to your words and your promises as I sat in my room quietly reading my Bible. I paid attention to the blowing of the wind and thought of you. Thank you, God, for this new day. I saw you as I received a smile from an elderly man who was disabled and in pain. I had the love and opportunity to return a smile as I opened the door for this fellow senior citizen. There are many ways I want to worship you. You see me. I am able to speak to you anywhere. I do not put limitations on where or when I speak to you, even as I drive in traffic. You hear my whispers. You hear any cry for help day and night. I honor you in reverence, God, and I thank you for your strength. Your strength is my joy. Loving you is my highest priority. You are vital through my life. You are sacred to me, Father. I love you. Shalom. Amen. Pour out your Holy Spirit, God," prays this Granny.

Question: Do you pray daily?

Here is my prayerful meditation: I pray, "Creator of the world, it saddens me that the atheist and secular world have become dominant in our society. Our Christian values are challenged in all aspects in the media. The people in the news and journalists who write newspaper articles are afraid to speak your name or pray. In my opinion, television shows and movies have become immoral when same-sex partner story lines are written as the norm today in most scripts shown daily. The offensive language and cursing, deliberate disrespect for women and men evident in the mean words spoken when talking to one another, usage of degrading dialogue to shock and awe the audience, award ceremonies and commercials paying celebrities that are not representing Biblical morals to our young children, preteens, and young adults, and adult situations within hearing range of our children most evenings before 9:00 p.m. The Internet and the various new and upcoming electronic devices are interfering and worshipped as material gods more than ever before, especially when people do not unplug in order to spend time and communicate with their family and friends. This Granny does ask you, God, to set our feet on your moral ground as once known and believed in the United States of America and around the world. I believe you, God, will bring these changes through each person's committed *collective consciousness*. I do see people giving of themselves more than in years before as seen through love in service to others through acts of kindness toward others during hurricanes, tornadoes, fires, floods, telethons, personal donations, illnesses, deaths, during random and senseless killings, and much more as mankind faces unexpected trails and tests that each us may face during this lifetime. We are becoming more aware of helping one another, loving one another, and connecting to one another. It warms my heart when I see Christ living through people. You living through us are our *hope* in the world today. Thank you hearing this grandmother's prayer, mighty God. Shalom. Amen."

God is not just on Sunday.

Question : Is the Father, the Son, and the Holy Spirit
thought about by you any other day
besides Sunday?

Here is my prayerful meditation: I pray, "Thank you for being available and my source of help twenty-four hours of each and every day, God. I need you. You are the answer to every problem I face on the earth. I am sorry that some of your children still do not know or accept you as their Father. I pray that by writing this book to *glorify* your name that *all* your children will seek and know you, Jesus. I heard your calling, and I obeyed. This is my testimony and witness to praise and to speak of my gratitude for *all* you have done for me. I am protected by your *grace, mercy,* and *favor*. Thank you for your many blessings, Father. Shalom. Amen."

Chapter Twenty-Six

The European Union

NO ONE KNOWS the end of time or knows how to interpret the book of Revelation. When I was younger, I heard we would have to learn the metric system because our money and our measurements were to follow the European market eventually. Because of the worldwide Unity Rallies, hacking, terrorism, and other world events I often hear people say that the world is going to hell in a hand basket. I was curious to find out historic events prior to my birth in 1951. In 1957, The Treaty of Rome dealt with economics between Germany, France, Italy, the Netherlands, Luxemburg, and Belgium. I wanted to mention this because the *euro* is an economic concern today with Greece, Spain, and Portugal. Had Brussels and Belgium removed their customs trade? Because of the recent hackings, I pray to God that we do God's will. The European Control Bank, *hopefully*, will not let the *euro* fail. What if the European Control Bank wanted to be united for economic, military, and political reasons? Will Britain remain or be left out, and will the United States be replaced as the super power?

We need to be on the watch for a religious leader who may or may not be a military leader or civilian leader. Let China, India, Brazil, and Russia be monitored, but this leader may or may not come from these countries. The leader will be more of a *Fascist*, and the leader will revive world domination concerning the military, communism, socialism, and will rule as a *totalitarian* state. There has been peace the last seventy years concerning the European world affairs. The United States will need to monitor these as Europe may or may not take over as the super power concerning population, domestic products, labor force, and the knowledge of many languages, but the United States may or may not have a slight edge concerning oil. Will the United States military ever join with the European military?

I wish I had learned more about Greek mythology in school. The eypo was the ancient coin of Greek and Roman leaders. Will Europe once again offer this coin for trade and for commerce through the European Union? Will this lead to civil authority through political and military power? Will the European police not just be British but French as well? As we learn about our *collective consciousness*, we are to be vigilant to these concerns addressed. This is mentioned by asking the question: Who are the wealthiest people running our world?

It is my curiosity to ask God in prayer, "Who and what countries own the land within the borders of the United States? Who are we in debt to and why? Who makes the higher man-made decisions for our country other than the president? Who do we believe concerning global warming? What truths are read in the daily newspapers and heard on the news? How private are our private lives?"

These questions are not out of fear. I converse with God about any and *all* of my questions.

I wonder why the people of the world tolerate and are tormented by such tyranny, whether it is a world leader or a country. It is God's power and authority that I *hope*, believe, and trust to see as we possibly face any trials, tests, and tribulations ahead. God is in control. Amen.

Acknowledgements

This book would not have been possible without the help from some very special people. John Koehler, my publisher, for your encouragement and guidance throughout this process. Thank you for your support and expertise. Lynda Gorniewicz, my editor, in making a disarranged manuscript into a final project. Eileen Ridge, my computer expert, your help was invaluable. Thank you from the bottom of my heart. And most of all to our *Lord* and *Savior, Jesus Christ*, for the ultimate demonstration of your unconditional love on Calvary, so our sins are forgiven.

CPSIA information can be obtained
at www.ICGtesting.com
Printed in the USA
FFOW03n1935040915
16484FF